CISTERCIAN STUDIES SERIES: NUMBER ONE HUNDRED EIGHTY-TWO

Enzo Bianch

PRAYING THE WORD
An Introduction to *Lectio Divina*

CISTERCIAN STUDIES SERIES: NUMBER ONE HUNDRED EIGHTY-TWO

PRAYING THE WORD
An Introduction to *Lectio Divina*

by

Enzo Bianchi
of the Community of Bose

Translated by James W. Zona

Cistercian Publications
Kalamazoo, Michigan – Spencer, Massachusetts

© Translation, copyrighted by Cistercian Publications, 1998.

Translated from the Italian
Pregare la Parola: introduzione alla 'Lectio Divina'
Eleventh, revised edition, 1992
Turin: Piero Gribaudi Editore

Cistercian Publications Inc.

Editorial Offices
The Institute of Cistercian Studies
Western Michigan University
Kalamazoo, Michigan 49008

Available from booksellers and from

Cistercian Publications (Distribution)
Saint Joseph's Abbey
167 North Spencer Road
Spencer MA 01562–1233

Cistercian Publications (UK)
Mount Saint Bernard Abbey
Coalville, Leicester LE67 5UL

Available in Canada through
Novalis
49 Front Street East, Second Floor
Toronto, Ontario M5E 1B3

*The work of Cistercian Publications
is made possible in part by support from Western Michigan University
to The Institute of Cistercian Studies*

Library of Congress Cataloguing-in-Publication data appears on page 120.

Printed in the United States of America

Silent Word,
Word of words,
Word made flesh
Only You are the Word!

TABLE OF CONTENTS

THE CHURCH HAS ALWAYS venerated the divine Scriptures as she venerated the Body of the Lord, in so far as she never ceases, particularly in the sacred liturgy, to partake of the bread of life and to offer it to the faithful from the one table of the Word of God and the Body of Christ. She has always regarded, and continues to regard the Scriptures, taken together with sacred Tradition, as the supreme rule of her faith. For, since they are inspired by God and committed to writing once and for all time, they present God's own Word in an unalterable form, and they make the voice of the Holy Spirit sound again and again in the words of the prophets and apostles. It follows that all the preaching of the Church, as indeed the entire Christian religion, should be nourished and ruled by sacred Scripture. In the sacred books, the Father who is in heaven comes lovingly to meet his children and talks with them. And such is the force and power of the Word of God, that it can serve the Church as her support and vigor, and the children of the Church as strength for their faith, food for the soul, and a pure and lasting fount of spiritual life. Scripture verifies in the most perfect way the words: 'The Word of God is living and active' (Heb 4.12), and 'is able to build you up and to give you the inheritance among all those who are sanctified' (Acts 20:32; cf. 1 Thess 2:13).

Let all the Christian faithful, and especially those who live in religious life, go gladly to the sacred text itself, whether in the sacred liturgy, which is full of the divine words, or in devout reading, or in such suitable exercises and various other helps which, with the approval and guidance of the pastors of the Church, are happily spreading everywhere in our day. Let them remember, however, that prayer should accompany the reading of sacred Scripture, so that a dialogue takes place between God and man. For, 'we speak to him when we pray; we listen to him when we read the divine oracles.'

Second Vatican Council
Dogmatic Constitution on Divine Revelation,
'Dei Verbum' 21, 25

English translation by Liam Walsh OP, in Austin Flannery, ed., *Vatican Council II, The Conciliar and Post-Conciliar Documents,* Collegeville, Minnesota: Liturgical Press, 1975.

1

APPROACHING
THE WORD OF GOD TODAY

FTER SEVERAL CENTURIES in exile, the Word of God
has been re-established in its central place in the life
of the Church. This is indisputable. We might even
speak of a *rediscovery of the Word of God* on the part of the
faithful who for centuries had no direct contact with Scripture
and, because of this estrangement, no opportunity to draw on
God's Word for their faith life. While it is true that the Church
has always lived by the Word of God, that the clergy have
employed it, and that scholars have given some attention to
it, for most people the centrality of the Word was obscured
by a system of rigorous doctrinal meditations which were in-
terposed between holy Scripture—the only fundamental and
determining element of the Church's life—and the awareness
of the average believer.

At the grass-roots level many liturgical, biblical and ec-
umenical movements which preceded the Second Vatican
Council and prepared the way for it, may have freed the Word
beyond the expectations and intuitions of even the council fathers. In any case, today the exile of holy Scripture is over, and
we are witnessing an epiphany of God's Word in the christian
community. As a Church, we should rejoice in this and thank
the Lord for calling us back to his Word and presenting it to

us anew. I am personally convinced that among the Council's many accomplishments, restoring the Word to the people of God will turn out to be the greatest manifestation of God's glory. Now that the Word is once again at the center of the Church's life, it will energize a process which has for a long time been at a standstill: God's active judgement on our human history as well as God's judgement on the life of the Church itself—which has always been a sort of pilgrim in this world—both a communion of saints and a company of sinners journeying toward the kingdom. The Word is waiting for us to rediscover it as a living, active and dynamic reality capable of sustaining our faith and inspiring our lives, and also capable of passing judgement on our behavior as Christians who live in the company and history of the human family. It is waiting to be preached forcefully in all our christian assemblies; to be read, meditated on and prayed over by individual believers and small christian communities.

Even so, it must be said that in our day a good deal of confusion exists about how to approach Scripture. Some methods of approach are inadequate to the Word's reality and unfulfilling to a person who is seeking God's presence in it. These approaches threaten the Word's sovereignty, its centrality in the Church, and its spiritual fruitfulness.

One method of approach which seems inadequate comes from the welcome many preachers and many of the faithful have given the new lectionaries—the one for feasts and the one for daily use. Both of them, but especially the lectionary for feasts, have been put together with a spiritual understanding which deserves to be recognized. With their publication, however, the production of books and guides to help preachers and the faithful understand the Word has been so excessive and exaggerated as to begin to raise suspicions. First of all, all these publications induce, in both individuals and the community, a kind of inertia towards the Scriptures themselves. They exempt both the preacher and the hearer from any personal exertion. So we could say that all the aids and compendia and summaries which flood the market with pre-packaged homilies and prefab *lectiones divinae* paradoxically risk taking direct contact with the Bible away from people. They dispense us from the laborious but necessary tasks of preparing ourselves personally, discerning for ourselves the meaning of a text, and—most important of all—praying over the text. How can any reflection, quickly prepared and mass-produced by someone else, even an exegete or a theologian, become living words that can provide real nourishment for disparate Christians in local churches leading diverse lives? Aren't preachers embarrassed to proclaim someone else's thoughts about texts which they themselves have neither meditated on nor pored over nor prayed about? Then we hear them complain that today God's Word no longer touches the congregation, which seems to put up impenetrable barriers and walls. But what are we preaching? Is it still the Word of God at all, the active and effectual Word proclaimed by a preacher who is a faithful witness, who has sincerely tasted it and understood it and is not afraid of the difficulties it involves?

Those who preach the Word must remind themselves often and remain conscious of the names which Scripture assigns them: they are 'servants of the Word' (Lk 1:2), 'servants and witnesses to the events in which the Lord has been seen and those in which the Lord will be seen' (Acts 26:16), 'servants of Christ and stewards of God's mysteries' (1 Cor 4:1), and above all, they are described as those devoted 'to praying and to serving the Word' (Acts 6:1–4). This means that someone who would preach the Word cannot hurry through it, much less parrot some homiletic summary. Nor can a preacher try to make the Word speak by giving it some makeshift intellectual, psychological, or sociological meaning. Instead, the preacher should first read the Word and spend long hours meditating on it, and then *pray it* with the intention of being of service to it. If it is true, as Saint Peter says (2 Pt 2:19), that people are slaves to whatever masters them, then the preacher must be above all a servant of the

Word. Only in this way can our preaching echo the Word and reproduce it without distorting it. The preacher must seek freely, sincerely, and fearlessly to be the Word's mediator, to help those who are listening to understand the significance of a particular text by connecting that text with the whole biblical message. To comment upon the Bible good preaching uses the Bible itself.

It is a presumptuous clericalism that says, 'Scripture has nothing to say to you, so I will say. . . .' Anyone who preaches the Word should recognize without blushing that his or her own faith witness has limits, and so urge those who listen to lay aside their feelings of inadequacy and approach the text themselves. The listeners will then find themselves invited to interpret the Word for themselves and to decide for themselves how it applies to their present situation and how it incarnates itself in their daily lives. I believe that the words of Saint Ambrose to the Christians of his time still have an urgent and useful message today: 'Why not dedicate your free time to reading Scripture? Aren't you in conversation with Christ? Don't you visit with him? Don't you listen to him . . . ? We listen to Christ by reading the Scriptures!'[1]

Another problem in the way we use Scripture lies in the approach of the so-called base communities and parish groups which willingly draw upon the Word of God. Here, community provides a context for the Word, and the intention is that the reading should be the spiritual center around which we all gather in order to grow. The style is conversational rather than clerically dominated. But the dimensions of individual, personal listening and engagement with the Word are often shortchanged. People try to find in Scripture messages of maximum relevance for burning issues in the life of the group. Because of this, the choice of readings can become selective, and so the group's reading becomes sectarian and consequently dangerous. Peace, social justice, violence and non-violence, marriage, freedom and human rights: all these concerns seem to be so pressing that they justify a reading of the Word which is discriminatory, favoring some of its messages and taking no account of others which it contains.

Saint John Chrysostom faced this kind of selective use of the Word long ago and felt moved to intervene with harsh words: 'This is a lukewarm approach to the Word, for it does not proceed by reading Scripture in its entirety and then making a choice about what seems most clear and useful and what demands less attention. Rather, such heresies have been introduced by peoples' refusal to read the whole of Scripture and by the belief that there exist parts of Scripture which have primary importance and others which have secondary importance.'[2]

This way of 'nibbling' or 'picking' at the text is characteristic of an opportunist who seeks to promote some interpretation of the Scriptures in the light of socio-political problematics and worldly ideologies. No longer do we find the Word of God shedding in the conscience of the believer a clear light on the signs of the times. Instead we are left with an ideology which drives the Gospel in a certain direction and dignifies any and every historical event as 'a sign of the times' which should give currency and content to the Word. When we read the Word with so much reliance on our own preconceived ideas, moreover, we may actually hamper its power to reveal to us any of the real signs of the times. We may become less open to letting the Word confront us on any issue or judge us by any standard which we have not already decided on by some means other than Scripture. This brings back the old temptation of *divination*, except that nowadays people are reading into the Scriptures what they assume to be the signs of the times according to their ideology, definitions, and interpretations based on sociological and psychological theories.

In cases like this, there seems to be too little effort expended on making the Word of God become prayer. Frequent praying, conversing with God, vanishes to leave room for analyzing social situations. The risk in such a method of reading is that it may never go beyond thinking and remain merely intellectual. It may never possess the power to address the reader personally, to bring about the believer's conversion and growth into the spiritual stature of Christ. Discussions which use the Word of God as proof-texts for certain ideas often end up as 'collages'. Biblical verses, especially certain ethical texts in the Gospels, are pasted together in summary fashion and wind up sounding like a series of slogans. Such a reading is not broad enough and results in a biased and univocal interpretation of the Lord's words.

Confusion has also resulted from another kind of reading, one based on so-called 'meditation'. This method, found mostly in religious communities where the daily use of Scripture is customary, is a poor second to *lectio divina* which is based on the Church's very rich tradition of the life of prayer in its first fifteen centuries. Frankly, this type of meditation has been somewhat distorted by ignatian ways of seeing things and relies on a lot of intellectualizing and psychologizing. It fills the life of prayer with too much systematic theology and too much methodological complexity. This, with its strong emphasis on the believer's will power, can make a person feel less like a contemplative than an athlete in training. Yet this is the method commonly used in religious communities.[3] Unfortunately, this method too often turns out to be just a mental exercise focusing on feeling-laden reflections and the sort of thoughts which rouse our sensitivities: the 'effluvia' and 'devotiones' which are measured by the intensity of our emotional response. This kind of meditation, typical of the *devotio moderna*, is seriously flawed by being both anthropocentric and egocentric. It pursues an individualistic interiority and aims at a mastery over the movements of the heart. Be careful. This kind of egocentric spirituality is making a comeback today in an updated guise, but as a method or a technique it still leaves us locked inside ourselves and fails to liberate us. In former times, this type of spirituality spoke of 'movements of the heart'. Today we hear of practices like 'deep cleansing', 'getting in touch with one's deeper self', 'self-emptying'. Christians should keep a certain distance from these types of meditation. They have little to do with authentic meditation, which is always centered on God and Christ and never on the self alone.

Above all, authentic christian meditation is not done with a view to 'getting something in return'. If something good happens, that's a bonus. Meditation seeks only one thing: to grow in communion with God. We find this communion by setting the senses free, moving down into the depths of the heart in order to find the unity that is there—the source of being—and then acting in relationship to God. For we experience God as communion with an Other, and it is God who orients us and enlightens us. As Christians we must not end with the self alone and forget to fix our eyes on God!

It is a great misfortune that today the term *lectio divina* and its meaning are unknown to a large segment of those in religious life. It is thought of as a prayer-form appropriate only to a strictly monastic setting—benedictine and cistercian. The Benedictine Rule,[4] in its attempt to make religious life a *dominici schola servitii*, 'a school of the Lord's service', says that to meditate means to read and re-read the Word, to chew it over and murmur it, to ponder it and repeat it, to fix it in the mind and keep it in the heart. This is different from trying to arrive eventually at a discussion of it (*scholasticism*), or at a feeling (*devotio moderna*). Instead, *lectio divina* seeks to arrive at prayer (*oratio*) and at contemplation, and thereby at action (*opus Dei*). But *lectio divina* is not the privileged property of monks. No form of religious life should ever see itself as a separate body, distinguished from others by the particular tradition of its institute, as if certain prayer forms could compete and create problems of 'coexistence' with other prayer forms and particular devotions, (whether eucharistic adoration, meditation, mental prayer, or any others). *Lectio divina* is simply the practice of praying over Scripture in preference to any other spiritual or patristic text. It is explicitly conscious that the Word is central in the christian life, that the Word is sovereign over every form of religious life, and that the Word has a role in effectively renewing religious life because it provides the norm for every kind of christian prayer. A recurring danger in religious life is that people can easily get so lost in their many activities that they find themselves empty and lacking in sound motivation. *Lectio divina* can provide us with the consistent opportunity and necessary time to return to the essentials, to the cornerstone which is Christ, and to the search for God which is the real reason for religious life in the first place.

Finally, we should keep in mind that wherever *lectio divina* has not been put into practice in a serious and consistent way, or wherever there has been, or presently is, a lack of constant reference to the Bible, distortions like the following always proliferate: sentimental piety, dry theologizing (which is nothing but intellectual speculation), shifting interests and an overemphasis on the secondary and derived aspects of the christian message, a hardening individualism which loses all sense of community, a taste for novelty for novelty's sake, a loss of the stability which is nourished by tradition and an almost idolatrous pursuit of the 'signs of the times'.

The men and women who have visible roles of ministry in the Church must go to the Word, the source, through *lectio divina*. If they do not, they are liable to appear in their preaching, teaching and pastoral work as people who depend on manuals, people who rely on the sometimes groundless opinions of others, people who lack certainty and therefore see problems everywhere, people who are incapable of speaking a 'strong' word 'with authority', but who instead speak as the scribes did in Jesus' time (Mt 7:28–29), people who blush at the Gospel they proclaim (cf. Rom 1:16; 2 Cor 3:12; 4:2). Only listening to the Word, welcoming it, storing it and meditating on it can make persons into prophets, leaders whose choices can liberate themselves and the rest of us and can create a people whose faithfulness to the earth and to humanity bespeaks God!

Because all these forms of confusion exist, I thought of offering some basic points about *lectio divina*.

Where do I get these points? First of all, from the long tradition of *lectio divina* in both the Eastern and Western Church, especially in patristic writings; from my own experience of putting this method into practice; from the lived experiences of the members of my own community; and finally from a consideration of the circumstances of the average believer which will necessarily reflect the way in which he or she will approach the Word.

In our times, modern psychology and biblical psychology share some common ground and it has become easier to practice meditation according to the patristic method. Today we recognize what was already the biblical view, that the human person is not a soul and a body viewed dualistically but rather an integral human person, not a ready-made being that possesses a soul in some interior space but a being that progressively constitutes itself as a self by being placed in history.

The life of humankind together is also a history. This means that human persons become real in relation to other persons and society, that human persons define their selfhood on the basis of their actions and reactions, their interactions with the world. And so that aspect of spirituality which we are calling meditation is neither a descent into our deepest interiority nor an individual ascent towards some being which is totally other; it is a journey toward the God who lives in the world. Meditation exists in service of human persons; it should make human beings more human.

We have said that we should read the Bible as a living Word, seek out its meaning and search for its guidance in history, the life of the Church, and our own lives. The Word is the power of God (cf. Rom 1:16) and it judges every situation *today*. So then, how can we draw near the Word in such a way that we will catch not only the echo of the time when it was written but also the living message it holds for our lives today?

God spoke at a precise moment in history, in a particular place and in a certain culture. How can we uncover the relationship between the particularity of history and God's constant revelation? Being mindful of a few points may help to give us greater clarity as we approach the text.

First of all, remember that revelation has taken place *within history*. The message it contains has resulted from political, economic, and personal events, and the Scriptures are less concerned with delivering dogmatic propositions than with demonstrating and witnessing to the action of God. They speak of God's mighty deeds *propter nos homines*, on behalf of us humans.

Revelation happens in the *reading* of an historic event (see, for example, Ex 12:37 and Lk 24:2–3). The community and the prophet *meditate* on the event in faith and in the Spirit and discover in it God's intervention, which then becomes a cause for praise and *prayer* (see Ex 15:1ff and Lk 24:34).

The revelation which we approach in the Bible was born through a process very like that of *lectio divina*: *reading* (the event), *meditating* (on the event), *praying* (about the event) then became an enduring testimony in the Bible, enfleshed in language, incarnated as an historic word! Stay aware of this. We need to work out a way to interpret the Bible's written accounts in the light of our everyday experiences, to make distinctions between the provisional framing of God's message in particular historical circumstances and the constant revelation contained within the framework. But even this will not be enough if we do not attend to the fact that *the Word itself*, besides being historic, *has a history*.

The conversation between God and humankind necessarily takes place in time. This is no informative discourse which hands down propositions to us in a quantitative increase of truths. Rather it is a progressive assimilation and understanding on our part of the truth once given in a fundamental intuition. We must always go back to this basic logic, to this ongoing dialogue with God. In doing *lectio divina*, a method based on *reading*, (*lectio*), we believers—each in proportion to our own abilities and skills—have to begin by reading from an historical perspective and stretch ourselves to understand the distant world in which the biblical page was drawn, the questions of that time and the demands of faith it sought to address, the concrete situation which was the object of its reflection. But immediately after this, we should begin to seek a more *global* or *doxological* reading; that is, one which draws out the message entwined in those historic circumstances and places it now in the context of salvation history, of God's overall design and plan, along with all the other revelations.

I will therefore try to present *lectio divina* in a renewed form, and to suggest a method for it which will not be too absolute or rigid, for I am convinced that the process of listening and praying is different for everyone and that the Holy Spirit actually tailors a method to each person.

For a lot of people, the effort to 'pray the Word' becomes too great once their initial enthusiasm wears off. They get tired and feel incapable of praying. I do not pretend to know how to teach anyone to pray. I can only offer what I have learned up to this point in the hope that I will be able to continue my own efforts along with all those believers who love the Word (Ps 119:97) and strive to become 'servants of the Word' (Lk 1:12).

I will try to present *lectio divina*, the prayerful reading of the Word of God, in a way I make bold to call 'Trinitarian', because as Christians our prayer and our life are both Trinitarian. Are we not moved by the Spirit to seek Christ by contemplating the one God, the Lord of the universe?

Notes

[1] Saint Ambrose, *De officiis ministrorum* 1.20.88 (PL 16:50A).

[2] Saint John Chrysostom, *Sermo I in illud: 'Salutate Priscillam et Aquilam'* (Rm 16:3) (PG 51:187)

[3] In the present phase of renewal in religious life an explicit invitation to *lectio divina* has only come about among the mendicant orders and in a clear call at the thirty-first General Congregation of the Society of Jesus.

[4] RB 4.55–56; 48; 49.4.

2

THE WORD OF GOD

THE SCRIPTURES contain the Word of God. They have far greater significance for the spiritual life of human beings than any mere ideological exposition; they cannot be reduced to being a book containing a few inspired theological and catechetical passages. The Scriptures are God's message to humankind and to each human person. They are a call addressed to each individual so that he or she may know God personally through an encounter with Christ and live for him and no longer for self.

The Scriptures deliver the Word of God to us when, with the assistance of the Holy Spirit, we penetrate into their core when we read and welcome them in faith as the Word which comes from God and leads to God. Even with the advances in biblical research which have spread in our day among a broad spectrum of christian people, we must recognize that our modern approach to the Word is sometimes characterized by a certain sterility because it relies more on reason than on wisdom, more on speculative study than on participative knowledge, more on thinking than on praying.

When we approach the Scriptures with the aim of nourishing our spiritual life, we should be seeking, not a revelation of new ideas or an increase of knowledge, but a commitment between God as speaker and ourselves as listeners. Another word for this commitment resulting from our coming together with God is 'covenant'.

The Word of God is the means by which we live in God, so we call it 'the word of life'. Without it we can never become persons who bear within ourselves Christ's life, the divine life of the Trinity. The etymological root of 'word' (*dabar* in Hebrew) indicates the depth of things, that which is hidden in them. To speak means to give expression to what is within things, to make visible and to activate what is behind them; their most profound, dynamic reality, their true name, the name God calls them. When God speaks, things come to be. God causes things to emerge and gives a name to things (see Gn 1:5,8). God governs things and extends divine power over them so that they can realize their particular vocation. God's Word is effective and does not return to God without accomplishing all that God intended (Is 55:10–11 and Gn 1:1–31).

This hebraic vision is very different from what we are used to in a culture derived largely from the Greeks. In the hebrew mind the Word always has an effect. Never a static thing, the Word is powerful and active. Action is one of the constitutive elements of the Word.

And so, in the Scriptures we find more than long treatises on life or humankind or history. We find the deep reality in and behind all these things, the sovereign power which God alone can exercise. The Word of God is not just a book or a collection of words on paper. It is rather a *seed* (Mt 13:19) that contains life in itself (Dt 32:47) and within which life itself develops until it becomes the great tree of the Kingdom. The Word of God sprouts in history as it does in our personal life and in the lives of all human beings. It grows and fills reality itself with a new presence. Like food, it nourishes people who are willing to receive it and it makes them holy. It enlightens people (Ps 119:105) because it unveils the mystery of things. It confers wisdom on the simple (Ps 119:130) and it brings all things to their final fulfillment (see Jn 17:17; Acts 19:20; Heb 4:12; 1 Pt 1:23; Lk 8:11; Mk 4:13–20, 26–32).

God created all things by his Word. The Word was already at God's side before God began creation and when God created, the Word was with God as architect (Prov 8:30). The Word instilled its force into creatures as they came into existence and marked them with its own seal. The Word is God's instrument. God hurls it onto Jacob (Is 9:7) or into the world (Ps 14:15). It rushes upon us and transforms the human story into a story of salvation (Ps 19:5; Rom 10:18; 2 Thes 3:1).

The Word of God fills the universe. It is God's resounding 'yes' written into every creature. It is the unique source of all that lives. In the Word we came to be. In the Word we live and move and have our being (Acts 17:28). The Word guides the whole creation and can be found in each single creature. We sense the sound of the Word in life itself and, if we can overcome our blindness, we discover it as the true depth of all reality. Suddenly we stand before the Word as the Author of all that exists, who is nevertheless so humble as to share a meal sitting alongside us (Rv 3:20). In the Word, God constantly and universally feeds us all.

And this happens not only in the dynamics of the created universe, in which all things reach toward their ultimate fulfillment in God; it also happened when the Lord God became present among us, visible in Jesus Christ. Then the Word, the divine wisdom, which at creation began concentrating itself into the striving of all material being, incarnated itself and was born in the flesh of one man, who bears the name Jesus.

This universal Word allowed itself to be concentrated in the judaic revelation to Abraham, Isaac and Jacob. This heavenly Word came to settle in a city, Jerusalem, making its dwelling place among humans (Cf. Si 24:1–12). This Word drew near to us, was on our lips and in our hearts so that we might put it into practice (Dt 3:14). This Word is eternal, but it made itself subject to time in Jesus, a human being like ourselves: 'The Word became flesh and dwelt among us' (Jn 1:14). As Saint Ignatius of Antioch put it, 'The Word came down from its silence and what was hidden came among us'.[5]

Now that the Word has become a person, we know him by name. He is the mirror of God, the image of the invisible God (Ws 7:26; Col 1:15). And now that we know him, as Saint Augustine states, the Scriptures no longer contain anything that is not an echo of the Christ.[6]

Just as we cannot encounter God except in the Son (Mt 11:27), so we today cannot welcome any word from God which is not the same Word that God revealed to humankind from the time of Abraham to the visions of the Apocalypse, the Word to which Scripture bears witness. In fact, we must receive Christ in Scripture as we receive him in the Eucharist, because the Scriptures not only witness to him but also find their fulfillment and realization in him. This is what Saint Jerome clearly perceived when he said: 'We eat Christ's flesh and drink his blood in the Eucharist but also in our reading of Scripture,' and when he proclaimed: 'I believe the Gospel is the body of Christ'.[7] For this reason, 'we should approach the Scriptures as the flesh of Christ!'[8]

The incarnation of God's Word into human words is the same incarnation—accomplished completely in Jesus Christ—found at all levels of the economy of salvation. We find the same mystery in all the books of the Bible: in both the First and the New Covenant.

After all, Christ is the one Word which contains all God's revelation. Saint Paul (2 Cor 1:19ff) affirms that in Christ all God's promises have received their 'yes' and have come true. The God who spoke in many times and in many ways (Heb 1:1–12) is the One who has spoken to us definitively in these last times in Christ. Saint Irenaeus of Lyon was right when he said that the Christ 'assumed in himself the long story of humankind, obtaining for all of us the sum total of salvation'.[9] Whether we open the pages of the First or the New Testament, then, we find ourselves before only a single book, 'and that single book is Christ, because all divine Scripture speaks to us of Christ and in Christ all Scripture is fulfilled'.[10] If we read the Scriptures with this criterion as our standard, we become those people who have the veil removed from their faces (2 Cor 3:12 ff) and know how to perceive Christ in the Scriptures.

Nicholas Cabasilas speaks of the Scriptures as the 'representation of Christ'. By this he means that in the Scriptures Christ speaks for himself and in doing so he puts us to the task of satisfying our eyes and our hearts with his presence. Nicodemus the Agorite says that only when we learn how to move from the written words to the 'substantial word' will we receive the true benefit for which God gave the Scriptures to the Church.

So then, *lectio divina* is a way of seeking Christ, 'the One I look for in the books'[11] as Saint Augustine says. Origen speaks of *lectio divina* as consuming the broken bread[12] and Saint Gregory Nazianzen speaks of it as consuming the paschal lamb.[13]

Lectio divina means sacred or divine reading, but the translation certainly misses the richness of this term. It is far more than just reading, which is too superficial. It is less than study, which is too intellectual. It is different from meditation, which is too pietistic and centered in one's own will. Hence we prefer to retain here the latin term *lectio divina* or to translate it with 'the Word prayed' or with 'praying the Word'.

Notes

[5] Saint Ignatius of Antioch, *Ad Magnesios* 8 2 (PG 5:669. In this I am following my reading of the presentation of these editions in J. B. Lightfoot and J. R. Harmer, *The Apostolic Fathers* (London 1891) 114, and of D. R. Bueno, *Padres Apostólicos* (Madrid 1979) 463. See also, Ignatius, *Ad Ephesios* 19.1, (PG 5: 659): 'Mary's virginity and her giving birth were hidden from the prince of this world, as well as the death of the Lord, and because they are the three mysteries which roar so explosively they were accomplished in the silence of God', and 15.1 (PG 5:657): 'One Master alone spoke and everything was made and all that He made in silence is worthy of the Father'.

[6] Saint Augustine, *Enarratio in Psalmum* 139.3 (PL 37:1804); see also *Enarr. in Ps.* 61.18 (PL 36:742).

[7] Saint Jerome, *Breviarium in Psalmo* 147 (PL 26:1334B); and *In Ecclesiasten* 313 (PL 23:1092A). On the relationship between the Word

and the Eucharist, see also Saint Augustine, *In Ioannis Evangelium* 9.1–17 (PL 35:1458–1466); Saint John Chrysostom, *In Genesim* 6.2 (PG 54:607); Rupert of Deutz, *In Matthaeum* 5.6 (PL 168:1433A); Origen, *In Exodum* 13.13 (PG 12:391AB). This final text, in which Origen is commenting on Exodus 35:4–5, deserves to be fully quoted: 'Be careful to interiorize the divine words and to keep them within yourselves, for fear that you might let them fall from your hands and be lost. I want to use an example in exhorting you on this subject, an instance of the care you exercise in another religious practice. When you regularly assist at the divine mysteries, you know how carefully and respectfully you receive the Lord's body when it is distributed to you, for fear that even a crumb might fall and a little part of this consecrated treasure might be lost. You would even blame yourself —and rightfully so— if a fragment were lost through your negligence. Well then, since you exercise such precautions in regard to the Lord's body, how could you ever dream that negligence toward the Word of God would deserve any less severe punishment than negligence toward his body?'

[8] Saint Ignatius of Antioch, *Ad Philadelphenses* 5.1 (PG 5:700C).

[9] Saint Irenaeus of Lyon, *Adversus haereses* 3.18.1 (PG 7:932B).

[10] Hugh of Saint Victor, *De arca Noe morali* 2.8 (PL 176: 642CD). The same text continues: ' . . . this is why in reading the Scriptures we seek the words and the precepts of Christ: we already know his acts. It is these that provide us with a sense of being worthy to do what he has commanded and to receive what he has promised' (PL 176:642D).

[11] Saint Augustine, *Confessions* 11.2.3–4 (PL 32:810–811).

[12] Origen, *Commentariorum in Matthaeum series* 85 (on Mt 26:26f; PG 13:1734AB).

[13] Saint Gregory Nazianzen, *Oratio* 45.16 (PG 36:644f).

3

THE LITURGY OF THE WORD

NOW THAT WE HAVE these initial considerations about the spiritual significance of the Word behind us, perhaps it is appropriate for us to go over the only passage in the First Testament which speaks of *lectio divina*. Certain points will emerge from our reflection.

In the eighth chapter of the book of Nehemiah, an unmistakable theology of the liturgy of the Word catches our attention. There we find a description of the very first act of the Israelite community after their return from exile. On this day a new phase of history is beginning for all Israel, a time when God's people will feel the divine presence more fully through God's Word. A solemn liturgical gathering of all the people, not only the men but women and children as well, is held. This day is prophetic in that it highlights the priestly and prophetic role of all the people, not just the priests and Levites who are delegated to lead public worship. At this feast we find the first and only description of the construction of an ambo, a lectern for the person who is going to read the Scriptures publicly. After a solemn blessing (Neh 8:6) and an *epiclesis*—a calling upon the Lord's presence by the people—the reading begins. It proceeds continuously throughout the entire day, passage by passage. The hebrew words are translated for the people who know only Aramaic. Ezra and the Levites follow the reading with explanations and commentaries. Before the Word of God, the word of justice, the double-edged sword, what other reaction can the people have but awe? Like Isaiah, like any human being who has come into contact with the divine and perceives God's holiness, they sense that their lips are unclean (Is 6:5), for God's presence is felt more than ever when the Word touches and penetrates the hearts of believers. Weeping occasioned by the Word of God is for their health as a people. The seed sown in tears reaps a harvest of joy (cf. Ps 126:6). The very words console: 'Do not weep . . . , come, eat . . . , celebrate a feast because this day is holy to the Lord!' (Neh 8:10–11).

This chapter captures the characteristic features of Israel's new form of worship, which will become the *lectio divina* of the synagogue, the celebration of the Word of God performed locally, apart from the temple sacrifices in Jerusalem. Now it becomes possible for all the people to participate in worship. Each Sabbath the people will welcome Torah, the Word of God, in their own villages and will experience the continuity between faith and daily life. Even the smallest, poorest and most isolated towns will have the Word of God proclaimed in them.

Jesus too practised this form of prayerful reading in the synagogues of Capernaum and Nazareth and in the other synagogues of Galilee. And he deepened the method of *lectio divina*, not only because he is in himself the realization of all that the Scriptures describe, but because he refers the reading of God's Word *to today*. When Jesus reads the passage from Isaiah 61 in the synagogue, he applies it to his present time, and his listeners discover that this word of Isaiah which is centuries old finds its 'today' in Jesus' proclamation (Lk 4:16ff). The people stand awestruck before God's Word in their present experience. This is exactly what we must discover each time we do *lectio divina*. This is very different from the kind of study that sidetracks us into speculative or even archeological reflections. 'Today this prophecy is fulfilled' (Lk 4:21). Understanding the ancient words in this way makes them contemporary and real, and we understand what is meant by the Word of God in all its power! Jesus' statement, 'today this prophecy is fulfilled', does more than notify us that the prophecy has become real in him, it actually creates a new *today* for all those who believe in him. Every believer is priest, prophet, and king—with the essential and indispensable qualities needed for reading the Word—and has not only the right to do *lectio divina*, but the capacity to apply the text to their own lives 'today'.

In *lectio divina* our *prophetic* quality as believers is shown by our capacity to resonate with the words that come from God and to let them work in us, to allow the Holy Spirit to judge our hearts as we read and to let it penetrate to the core of some life situation where the Word itself will resound. Our *kingly* quality as believers is shown by our capacity to 'consecrate' history and to understand it as a history of salvation. Kings are anointed and consecrated on behalf of a whole people, and we the people are called to make the Word real in our history. Our *priestly* quality as believers is shown when we approach the Scriptures as a sacrament which symbolically establishes a contemporaneity between some historical event in the Bible and our lives today.

The Church is always concerned with 'today', because the Church is a community of people who are priestly, prophetic and kingly. Our first task as Church is to proclaim the Word, that is, to make the Scriptures real in the present. 'The Church conserves the Scriptures and understands them because it possesses the Spirit who has dictated them. In the Church Jesus creates the means by which he can teach. . . . The *didascalia* are Christ's own lips, his psalter, his doctrine'.[14]

Every time we celebrate the Liturgy of the Word and turn our eyes to the text, Christ explains it to our hearts in proportion to our faith. The Holy Spirit's power cooperates with the strength of our personal faith, the intensity of our personal prayer and the prayer we share with others. By these activities, Jesus makes the text become real for us. This is why a real commitment to prayer must precede *lectio divina*.

Reading commentaries is much less important than preparing our consciousness and opening our heart to the Scriptures. Then Christ will make himself present, and he himself will announce the Word and explain it to us. Deuteronomy says: 'Your eyes have seen the *words*' (4:9), and Isaiah speaks of 'having a vision of the Word of God' (2:1). Why these unusual expressions? How can we 'see' and 'have a vision' of a word which by nature ought to be heard? Because the word is God's Word and we are listening in faith, we can receive it in our deepest being and see in a kind of interior vision all that it truly is: the Word of God judging us, inviting us, leading us into mystery, disposing our wills to be totally centered in Christ. Not only is Christ present, Christ is heard, and the same Christ is seen. Some hearers have spiritual eyes that see as well as hear. Why should this capacity be thought of as anything less than that of listening? 'Hidden in the words of Scripture we find the Kingdom of heaven. It is unveiled to those who persevere in prayer with peaceful hearts, praying over the psalms and the readings and all those words that normally enlighten the spirit.'[15]

Notes

[14] See Origen, *In Evangelium secundum Matthaeum* 14.6 (PG 13: 1198).

[15] Nilus, *Epistola* 3295 (*Didymo lectori*; PG 79:529CD).

4

FROM THE LITURGY OF THE WORD
TO *LECTIO DIVINA*

WHY DID THE WORD OF GOD address the biblical authors? Was it so that it could be fixed in writing and become a written code for the faithful? Even more, was it not so that the written Scriptures might always become Word when they are proclaimed to us?

The liturgy is the privileged place where Scripture becomes Word. The chapter of Nehemiah we looked at earlier as well as Saint Luke's passage about Jesus' presiding at the synagogue service in Capernaum witness to this. The Word of God comes alive in the liturgy and is effective because Christ is present, proclaiming it with his own voice. It becomes much more than a simple document.

In addition to manifesting the unity of God's people, the liturgical assembly is the visible sacrament of the Word—to use a definition of Saint Augustine. In the assembly, the Word makes itself heard sacramentally. It is Christ himself who speaks when the Scriptures are read aloud in church; Christ acts and works through his Word. By a remarkable spiritual instinct, the byzantine liturgy, just before the proclamation of the Gospel, has the deacon raise the sacred book aloft and exclaim: 'Be attentive to the wisdom of God', or in other words: 'Pay attention; God is speaking'. In its proclamation the Word comes, and comes with God's creative power.

The entire New Testament unanimously witnesses to this. Saint Paul writes to one of the assemblies: 'In receiving the Word of God as we preached it, you have welcomed it as God's own Word. That is what it really is, not the word of human beings. It is capable of exercising its power in you who believe' (1 Thes 2:13).

The assembly's faith, the first sign of the Word's effectiveness, is born from the Liturgy of the Word, just as the liturgy in turn is born from the Word of Christ (See Rom. 10:17).

Origen, in commenting on this passage, makes the claim that Christ can be heard speaking directly in three modes: he was heard as a man by eye witnesses; he was heard in the preaching of the apostles; and he is heard in the heart of everyone who listens to him. All three modes are real ways of listening to the Lord.

The liturgical assembly is more than a gathering of believers. These believers have been made priests and prophets and are capable of reading and listening to the Scriptures with the lively spirit of priests and prophets. Because of these qualities which the assembly possesses as Church, each single member can make the Word come alive both for his or her individual benefit and for the whole Church.

At the same time, 'no word of Scripture is a matter for private interpretation' (2 Pt 1:20). The guidance offered by the Word in the context of the liturgical celebration always takes first place. Any personal *lectio divina* must find its ultimate meaning in the Liturgy of the Word. *Lectio divina* should both prepare for the liturgy and be a continuation of it. If we seem to be stressing this primacy of the Liturgy of the Word over every personal contact with Scripture, there are essential and indispensable reasons for it:

First of all, there surely exists a *direct Word of God*, implicit in the Scriptures but addressed to us personally outside of Scripture. It is a Word from God which we perceive in a personal way and which will never become a written word, but it is nonetheless God's Word. The condition for the arrival of God's personal message to each of us is that we possess an aptitude for listening carefully to the liturgical Word. When Saint Paul writes: 'Insofar as brotherly and sisterly love is concerned, it is not necessary for me to write to you, because you have learned from God himself to love one another' (1 Ti 4:9), and when Saint John says: 'It is written in the prophets: they will all be taught by God,' (Jn 6:45), they reveal the possibility that the Word of God may be addressed directly to an individual. Even so, is the privileged place for this personal hearing not the Liturgy of the Word within the assembly? Surely, all who know the Scriptures are promised this personal kind of knowledge, but it springs from the community's practice of preaching and from the liturgical celebration of the Word.

Another reason for the importance of *lectio divina* is that it *prepares us for the liturgy*. If the Word is received without preparation, without faith, love or attentiveness, it no longer gives life. It will be for us a dead word. For our hearing and interpretation of the Word is to be 'doxological'—that is, if the criterion is to be commentary on the Word by the Word—it is necessary to have that profound knowledge of the Word which is possible only through loving and constant study of it. The passages chosen by the Church for the lectionary provide a minimum for living the faith. We need to be familiar with the *whole* Word even to understand those passages deeply. Knowing enough Scripture means that the proclamation of any particular liturgical reading will resonate in the believer and call to his or her mind all the texts and all the theology it suggests. In short, the believer should become a 'living concordance' of the Scriptures.

But this is not only a matter of gaining a broader and deeper knowledge of Scripture; it is also a matter of personal appropriation. God speaks to the whole people in the liturgy, but this is only the beginning and the cause of what must become a personal encounter with God. In the text, God may be calling Abraham or Moses, but this voice must begin to call *me* and repeat *my* name. When God changes a person's name in the Scriptures, I have to feel within myself the change the text suggests. The dialogue which takes place between God and the whole people in the liturgy must become a unique and personal dialogue for the individual in *lectio divina*.

It is a little too simplistic to say that in the liturgical sphere the Word announces theological and catechetical truths, whereas in *lectio divina* these truths become personal and spiritual. How forcefully Origen knew how to make the Word personal! Look at the daring with which he calls himself the church, and even the bride! 'I, the church' he says of himself,[16] just as Saint Bernard would later proclaim, 'Each of us is the church!'[17] A canon of the council 'in Trullo' prescribed that priests should not only preach the Word in the liturgy, but should continually teach the faithful to be intimately familiar with Scripture, so that 'they will use the means that the Bible provides to become mature Christians'.[18]

So *lectio divina* is not the specialty of monks. It exists for the whole Church. It is the necessary condition for the Word to bear fruit in us. Let's not deceive ourselves: anyone who tries to live only on the liturgical proclamation of God's Word is like the soil in Christ's parable which welcomes the seed but bears no fruit. This kind of person is like arid land. The birds eat the seed. The thorns suffocate it. The heat dries it out as it sprouts. Saint John Chrysostom vigorously insists on this point when he appeals to the people in these words: 'Some of you may say, "I am not a monk . . ." But here you are mistaken, because you think that the Scriptures are meant only for monks, whereas they are actually far more necessary for you, the faithful who live in the midst of the world. The only thing more gravely sinful than not reading the Scriptures is believing that reading them is useless and serves no purpose.'[19] This great church father goes so far as to say that the person who lives without doing *lectio* engages in a 'satanic practice'. Once heard, the Word must speak unceasingly. It must be stored up and continually reawakened in the heart. How can we have any spiritual life if the Word does not breathe within us day and night?

Saint John Chrysostom was a pastor responsible for the church in his care. He constantly struggled against the temptation of requiring the radical practice of the Gospel only from his monks. He frequently admonished the faithful to continue the Liturgy of the Word in their *lectio divina*. 'When you return home you should take the Scriptures and, with your wife and children, you should read and repeat together the Word you have heard [in Church]',[20] and again, 'Return home and prepare two tables, one with plates of food, the other with plates of Scripture. Let the husband repeat what was read in Church. . . . Make your house into a church'.[21]

Hearing the Word of God superficially is always a dangerous trap. The Word we hear is like the seed broadcast by the sower: having once heard it, we must struggle against the devil who can come along and steal it from us or sow weeds around it. So try not to hear the Word superficially (like the seed along the wayside), not to be overcome by the difficulty of conserving it (like the seed on stony ground), not to be afraid to let it grow (like the seed sprouting among the thorns) (See Mt 13:18 ff and 13.24 ff).

To be able to say like Origen, 'I, the church', to have his ecclesial spirit, we need to read Scripture. The Scriptures render a person *theodidactus*, 'taught by God', in the words of Saint Clement of Alexandria.

Above all, keep in mind that in *lectio divina*, prayer is personal, but not private or individualistic. The 'reading' is 'divine' because it is read in dialogue with God, the Other. The two of you read together.

Because the Scriptures are God's message to humankind, they either become a conversation with God or they remain fruitless. We can read *about* God in Scripture, or we can read the Scriptures with faith and pray them, aware that God is a 'You', Someone who stands before me, who speaks to me and listens for my answer. This is the final result of *lectio divina*. The message proclaimed about God becomes personal to me and in praying over that message I speak to God. Listening to the Word, we listen to God. Praying, we speak to God.

Notes

[16] Origen, *In Canticum Canticorum Homelium* 17 (SCh 37bis:95). We must emphasize, however, that these words are placed in the mouth of the Church: 'I, the Church; I, the bride; I, the spotless one have been appointed keeper of many vineyards by my mother's (that is, the synagogue's) sons, who had once fought against me'. (This is a reference to Saint Paul.) But it is well known that for Origen, 'the Church is the assembly of all the holy ones. It is therefore like a single person formed from the gathering of many' (*In Canticum Comm.* 1; PG 13:84C). And in the middle of that same *Commentary on the Canticle*, Origen identifies 'the bride, that is, the Church or the soul which is striving toward perfection' (*In Canticum Comm.* 3; PG 13:159B). Thus he links the Church to the faithful soul: 'So you too, insofar as you are Church, can direct your words at the daughters of Jerusalem' (*In Canticum Canticorum Hom.* 1.6: SCh 37bis:91). Origen can then exhort: 'Let us also build a sanctuary to the Lord, all of us together and each one individually. The sanctuary which we will build is the Church, holy, spotless and without wrinkle . . .' (*In Exodum* 9.3: SCh 16:211).

[17] Bernard of Clairvaux, *In Cantica Sermo* 57.3, (PL 183:1051B); see also Sermon 68.1 (PL 183: 1108C): 'We are the bride'; and the very beautiful text that ends Sermon 12, in which Saint Bernard reworks the passage that applies the term 'bride' to the Church to apply to the individual soul.

[18] See John Chrysostom, *In Epistolam ad Ephesios Commentarius* 621.1–2 (PG 62:150–151).

[19] Saint John Chrysostom, *In Matthaeum* 25 (PG 57:30).

[20] Saint John Chrysostom, *In Matthaeum* 51 (PG 57:55f).

[21] Saint John Chrysostom, *In Genesim* 62 (PG 54:607). See Canon 19 of the Council 'in Trullo': 'Pastors of the church ought to instruct the people every day, but above all on Sunday, they should also explain the Scriptures utilizing the commentaries of the Fathers'.

5

FORMATION IN *LECTIO DIVINA*

ONE OF THE GRAVEST admonitions repeated by the fathers is against profaning the Scriptures by making them an object of speculation or of knowledge for knowledge's sake, something even an atheist can do. A believer, on the other hand, should know that when we hold the Scriptures in our hands we can understand what we read only by the grace of God. *Lectio divina*, therefore, is the most authentic and appropriate way to read the Scriptures and to receive God's grace through them.

The rabbis used to say that the Torah, the Word, was God's presence in creation, a presence that people could appropriate by *reading*, *meditation* and *prayer*. These are the three fundamental moments of *lectio divina* in jewish, as well as in the most ancient christian, piety.

This jewish method of assimilating the Word was inherited by Christianity (see 2 Tm 3:14–17 and Rom 15:4) and was shared by all the Fathers of the Church, in both East and West, even though it was fully elaborated only in the Middle Ages.[22] Later, especially in the sixteenth century, *lectio* fell into disuse in the Church. Yet it survived in a different form in the Reformed Churches. Their experience can certainly help us to mark the breadth of *lectio divina* and the various ways of doing it set out by the ancient fathers and enriched by the medieval fathers. In monasteries, however, the practice of *lectio* was preserved without interruption and often provoked polemics against other ways of reading Scripture. The critical confrontation came in the Late Middle Ages between Canons Regular and certain Dominicans whose scholastic *lectio* tended in the direction of *quaestio* and *disputatio*, and not toward the ultimate good of *meditatio* and *oratio*.[23] Still later, *lectio* conflicted with the very psychological and introspective ignatian method of meditation. Even within monasticism, *lectio divina* had to be defended against a twelfth-century tendency to subject it so completely to liturgical prayer that it was reduced almost to non-existence amid the endless offices which the *opus Dei* substituted for *lectio*.[24]

Doing away with *lectio* as a method was equivalent to doing away with the Word itself. Recently, however, the Second Vatican Council offered the Word to us again: 'It is necessary that everyone . . . immerse themselves in the Scriptures by constant *sacred reading* . . . by diligent *study*, . . . and let all remember that *prayer* should accompany the reading of sacred Scripture'.[25]

Lectio divina—prayerful reading or praying the Word or meditative prayer—is still a method privileged by the Church, and we would here like to offer a few introductory lines about it.

In studying the various phases of *lectio divina* and getting to the heart of it, we have the guidance and help of Guigo II the Carthusian, who in one of his invitations to *lectio*, applied to one of Jesus' sayings on prayer this method which he himself had worked out in *The Ladder of Monks*.[26]

In the Gospel according to Saint Matthew 7.7, we find the following words of Jesus: 'Ask and it shall be given to you, seek and you shall find, knock and it shall be opened to you'. Guigo paraphrases this, saying: 'Seek by reading and you shall find in meditation. Knock in prayer and contemplation shall be opened for you to enter'.[27] Guigo summarizes the method of *lectio divina* in terms of the last two gospel invitations. We think the first invitation can also be paraphrased:

'Ask and you shall receive,' could mean 'Ask the Holy Spirit and you shall receive the capacity to read'.

In Guigo's words, we find a step-by-step plan for formation in *lectio divina*. All our spiritual energy is directed toward arriving at true prayer, at our face-to-face encounter and communion with God. A plan like this is helpful for both our reading and our prayer. It is especially instructive during our first efforts.

ASK THE HOLY SPIRIT AND YOU SHALL RECEIVE ENLIGHTENMENT

Before reading Scripture, Saint John Chrysostom always prayed: 'Open the eyes of my heart so that I may know and do your will . . . , enlighten my eyes with your light'. Saint Ephrem the Syrian gives this advice: 'Before you read, pray and implore God to reveal himself to you'.

This is the first and fundamental attitude for anyone who approaches *lectio divina*, to ask the Spirit of God to come and enlighten our whole being and to make possible an encounter with the Lord. We live in a condition of blindness and we must cry out before the holy Book, 'Lord, that I may see', and 'Lord, open the eyes of my heart', in the same way as both the hebrew and roman liturgies have us pray, 'Lord, open my lips' before we can even praise God. Every reading of the Scriptures presupposes an *epiclesis*—a calling down of the Lord's Spirit—because the Scripture becomes a living word only through the Spirit who fills it and only because the Spirit rests upon it as it rested upon the Son at his baptism.

In reading, we seek the spiritual or pneumatic dimension of a passage, the dimension where we will encounter the body of Christ, the Church, and the tradition in which the Word speaks. The Church is a body in which the divine words echo forth as words of life. The Church does not possess the Word so much as have custody of it because of the Spirit who dwells within both the Church and the Scriptures. So the *epiclesis* is a calling out to the Spirit in union with the Church. In the liturgy, the gathering of the people itself can be said to be an *epiclesis*, but in *lectio divina* each believer must call out for the Spirit in union with that great eucharistic *epiclesis* in which the Church continually cries out in her total and substantial communion with Christ, her spouse. In this way, we avoid the danger of using the Word of God in an exclusive way and of creating interpretations which are overly subjective or fantasies which are self-serving. The individual believer's approach to the Word becomes a sacrament, in which the Church and Scripture are united as a single source of the Word of God.

We may ask God for the Spirit confident that we shall receive it, because this is the one prayer that we know will always be heard. The Spirit is the 'good gift' which the Father can never deny to his children (see Lk 11:13).

The Holy Spirit did not act just once through the authors who wrote the holy Scriptures. The Spirit still acts in persons who read the Scriptures, and only the Spirit's presence can ensure that the letter of Scripture will be constantly freshened and renewed to become spirit for the reader. The Scriptures become the life-giving Word only when God's Spirit energizes the person reading them.[28]

It is the Spirit who guided the writing and the Spirit never abandons the Word as it enters the history of the world. Rather the Spirit makes it a Word of life for those who will listen to it. Without the *epiclesis*, we will not find God's Word contained in the text. It is revealed in proportion to the openness and receptivity of the reader to it. Saint Gregory the Great says that 'the same Spirit which moved the souls of the prophets moves the heart of the reader',[29] and Saint Ephrem states clearly that 'only when we are filled with the Spirit can we drink in Christ'. William of Saint Thierry taught that 'the Scriptures need to be read by the light of that same Spirit in which they were written and understood in that light'.[30]

So the *epiclesis* produces in us first of all receptivity, then compunction and enlightenment.

We should seek to cultivate the attitude of receptivity, but it depends on the Spirit. It is a kind of synergy between our human will and the Spirit's activity. This openness to the Spirit has been much ignored until now in the theology of the West, which has never given great emphasis to an understanding of the Spirit's role in the life of the believer. And yet, it is an essential disposition if we seek something more than listening to a dead letter or, more aptly, if we seek to listen in a way that is more than purely intellectual and speculative.

Lectio divina is not just taking an interest in knowing the books of the Bible. It is a reading of those books done by two persons, the reader and the Spirit. We cry out, 'Come, Lord!' And only then does Christ emerge from the text to be seen by the eyes of faith. Our receptivity welcomes the Spirit. A monk of Mount Athos quite properly compared the gentle reverence and respect we should have in our attitude toward the Spirit with the way we would treat a dove. The quieter, the stiller we stay quiet, and the more we give it our careful attention, the closer to us it will come.

The coming of the Holy Spirit, for which we prepare by prayer and receptiveness, produces detachment. This is a 'letting go' that takes place within us. We cannot listen attentively to the Word of God if we do not quiet what is going on inside us. We cannot give our attention to reading if the center of our attention is our ego. We cannot be free for God's action in us if we cling to ourselves and do not abandon ourselves totally to him.

We should therefore make an effort to reject our illusory needs, our latest idols, the false gods which we daily invent. Really, it is society that convinces us that we need so many things. Advertising and the subtle suggestions of a consumerist culture create needs in us. When people confess that they are not finding 'satisfaction' in reading the Scriptures, I often ask myself if it is because they are approaching the Word in an attempt to satisfy some specific need they have. Are they expecting results from the Word that it will not give them because, like prayer, the Word is not up for sale? It takes effort to detach oneself from one's own interior conversation, one's own interior agenda, and to try to abandon one's egocentricity to seek and to listen only to God.

This is a very simple but basic requirement which must be stressed especially in our day and age, for our frantic rhythm of life and the general callousness that results from it can be a difficult obstacle when we try to enter naturally into this dimension.

If we find that we cannot empty our consciousness by our own efforts, we would do well to follow the advice of Pachomius: 'Let us slow down the confusion caused by the many thoughts which torture us and which bubble up in our hearts like boiling water by reading the Scriptures and reflecting on them constantly . . . and we will be freed. . . .'

Among the Hebrews the posture for prayer was raising the hands upwards, a gesture which symbolized this detachment by focusing attention on what is above us. 'To you, O Lord, I lift up my soul!' (Ps 25:1). Think of the exclamation *sursum corda*—'Lift up your hearts'—in the roman liturgy and the hymn of the cherubim in the byzantine liturgy. They act as a summons to us to go out of ourselves and to concentrate on Christ. 'Let us lift up our hearts and our hands toward the God who is in heaven' (Lam 3:41).

We should strive with our whole being toward the Most High or rather, we should let ourselves be carried aloft by the Word. This attitude, 'need not evoke any feeling of sublimity, much less of self-importance, but should be cultivated in the deepest humility and poverty of spirit'.[31] When we speak of lifting up our hearts we mean focusing our attention on God, and not being carried away by our feelings. Saint Augustine aptly observes that: 'The heart does not rise aloft the way a body does. A body changes its location, but for a soul to rise aloft it is enough that it change its will'.[32] Lifting up our hearts, then, means that we enter into the field of the attraction which God exerts on us. We let ourselves be drawn by the Spirit, gathering up and focusing every scattered aspect of our being on God and on the text we are considering in our *lectio divina*. Lifting up our hearts means going to God by our loving awareness. It is more than lifting up our minds, more than meditation understood as a merely human effort. Loving awareness comes from the heart; it is a relationship of heart to heart, of one person to another. And the expression 'heart to heart' does not have to be understood romantically, but may signify that attitude which John the beloved disciple had in his intimate conversation with Jesus as he reclined on his chest. Origen calls this 'appreciating the deeper meaning of the Gospels'. To sum up, then, receptiveness leads us to lift up our hearts and this focuses our attention.

Attention means an attitude of listening to the Lord who wishes to speak to us. We give attention not only to the message, but to Him who gives the message. Mary Magdalene gave her attention to the gardener when he called her by name and she came to perceive the presence of the Lord and saw Jesus (Jn 20:15–16). What God really requires of us in this mysterious dialogue is first and foremost that we be attentive listeners. Then the communication between the person who prays in faith and the Word will become mysteriously intimate and our whole humanity will be brought into the presence of God. Saint Ambrose described attention as 'the whole person being intensely involved in the act of listening to God.'[33] Person meets Word. J. A. Bengel, the protestant theologian, neatly summed up our attentiveness to Scripture when he wrote: 'Give yourself over wholly to the text, and apply the whole text to your life!'

We must not become slack about listening to the Word, because as Caesarius of Arles wrote: 'Someone who listens to the Word half-heartedly deserves the same blame as someone who negligently lets the Lord's body drop on the street.'[34]

If our attention is thorough and our surrender complete, we find it easy to cling to God fully, because as Saint Gregory the Great put it, we find ourselves 'suspended in the love of God'.

Let me repeat this for emphasis. These dispositions of the soul are necessary, but it is only when the Spirit gives them life that they can be used to achieve the full scope of *lectio divina*. If we call upon the Spirit in addition to having the proper dispositions, we will surely receive the enlightenment required to read the Scriptures successfully.

SEEK BY READING AND YOU SHALL FIND IN MEDITATING

To accept the truth that praying is important leads to the conclusion that reading the Scriptures is equally important. According to John Cassian, reading brings us understanding and a certain comprehension, an intimate familiarity with the Word. But before we talk about the activity of reading as one phase of *lectio divina*, we should establish certain guidelines so that our practice of reading may be authentic.

First of all, our reading should always take place at a fixed time. The believer must exercise some discipline in this regard, to find what is the most suitable time for reading. The time of day will vary from person to person, but what is important is consistency. A specific set time is necessary because as humans beings we are limited and can only successfully do one thing at a time. Focusing on one task will destroy our focus on something else. It cannot be over-emphasized that sufficient time is needed for reading Scripture and that a time should be deliberately chosen—at night, in the morning, at sunset—always a time that favors calm, quiet, and solitude. Let's not forget that there are obvious external ways to help our spirit be more attentive.

'Why then does one seek after such a great love, since what one seeks to find one finds in the seeking? Because when one seeks to find an ever greater sweetness, one can find it only by seeking with an ever greater desire'.[35]

William of Saint Thierry in his *Golden Epistle* advises us always to do our reading at a set time: 'At fixed hours time

should be set aside to do definite reading. Haphazard reading, constantly varied and spontaneously chosen, not only
fails to edify the soul but actually robs us of our stability'.[36]
We cannot simply clip off pieces of time for our reading. Like
prayer, it can never be just a way of passing the time. Certainly
in this age of frenetic activity the believer is sorely tempted to
relegate reading Scripture to the left-over times of the day.
But by restricting our reading to times that are not conducive
to it, we will not be able to reap the fruits we were hoping for.
Without the exterior quiet and the recollected spirit of a person
'who enters into their own room and shuts the door and reads
in secret' (Mt 6:6), it is just not possible to give our attention
to God. Jurieu says frankly: 'The exchange between a soul
and its God happens in secret', and Saint Jerome counsels:
'Always maintain the mystery of your own interior room, so
that the Bridegroom can live there. Then when you pray you
will speak to him and when you read Scripture he will speak
to you'.[37]

We need have no fear that we will be left alone perma-
nently. 'Progress in the spiritual life requires the discipline of
a life in community but the Lord is known and tasted in secret
times of silence'.[38]

In solitude we are prepared to enter into God's world
and to sense how close God is to us. 'You are near, O Lord!'
(Ps 119:151). There will be times when we are aware of God's
presence, sometimes only with difficulty but at other times
easily and with enthusiasm (See Ps 84). Sometimes we will
feel that we can hold our heart in our hands and that we can
place ourselves in the hands of God, or on God's chest, or
under God's wings (Cf. Pss 61:5 and 91:4).

Experiencing this, we cannot help but be filled with both
joy and fear. Fear means here not being frightened of God's
severity, but a sense of human smallness and contrition for
one's imperfections. It is a spiritual sense, not a sentimental
feeling. Sometimes we are able to experience compunction,
like the people who wept when Ezra read the Scriptures to
them. The gift of tears is one of the Spirit's riches, so rich in fact

that the medieval fathers often commended it. Isn't this kind of weeping—which arises from our compunction and shows itself in the visible sign of tears—really the spiritual groaning which the Spirit produces in us (Rom 8:26)? Whenever the Spirit granted Saint Romuald of Ravenna an understanding of the meaning of some passage of Scripture, his eyes would fill with tears because the Bible was showing him its secret treasures.[39] And Saint Gregory the Great gives this description of the monk who knows how to assimilate the Word of God: 'Often I have seen people who are so dedicated to *lectio divina* that they offer a sacrifice of tears to the Lord, and in their tears they offer themselves as victims. Their heart is so full of the Bible and their interior so saturated with the Word of God that their soul is always recollected, and their tears show their holy awareness of God'.[40] This is the way we should open the Bible, with respect and reverence, with an *epiclesis* and with compunction.

And if it is true that we should do our reading at set times, it is also true that we should plan which specific passages we will read. It is not advisable, or even possible, really, to page through the Scriptures once in a while, whimsically turning from one passage to another. Having a daily lectionary with the readings set out is a grace for this very reason. It invites the Christian to read consistently and in some order. Only reading the Bible in sequence can surpass this practice. Looking around for passages that suit our moods is reducing the Bible to a book in which we search for what we want to find. Instead of this, we should take the text on its own terms and not choose passages according to our own preferences, even though at times our preferences may seem justifiable for personal or collective reasons. When we read, we should try to put aside our own bias and allow ourselves to be drawn obediently to where the Spirit wants to take us.

Opening the Scriptures and reading, according to Saint Jerome, is 'opening our sails to the Holy Spirit without knowing on what shores we will land'.[41] We cannot afford to let ourselves be carried away by our craving for novelty or by our idle curiosity when we stand before the Scriptures containing God's message. This book speaks on its own terms, by the grace of the Holy Spirit, and we should guard against trying to make it say what pleases us. Saint Augustine said, 'God seeks not your words but your heart!'[42] Of course, we are all tempted to choose texts which will produce exalted feelings but we should not forget that the real benefit of God's Word is that it is our daily bread. Like all healthy nourishment, it cannot always satisfy all our tastes and appetites, though occasionally it is particularly enjoyable.

Drawing near the Scriptures in faith also means being ready to hear some messages which are difficult to penetrate, some that seem strange or demanding, messages which at first seem as if they could not possibly apply to me. A particular text may seem to 'say nothing to me'. The dialogue of friendship takes place not only in an exchange of words but also in moments of silence, which God can use to speak to us eloquently about our emptiness in contrast to the divine fullness shown to us in Scripture. These moments can also speak to us about our need to surrender radically to the text. 'Apply yourself totally to the text.' Then we will frequently find that 'the whole meaning applies to you!' These silences are often helpful, even though they may seem to signal dryness and spiritual boredom. They help us to fix our attention completely on God, to concentrate on our reading of Scripture, and to praise God in that silence which alone can remind us that by ourselves we are finally not capable of praying. God fills our silence, just as he filled the mouth of the psalmist and blessed his lips (Ps 81:11).

We may also find ourselves running up against obscure passages and difficult words, as, for example, the odd language of Balaam where he speaks of God as 'the buffalo's horn' (Nm 23:22), or the messages that come in the flames on Sinai or at Pentecost. These are images and when we read or recount them they are meant to produce in us not logical thinking but love and the sense that here is a message which will overwhelm us. Saint Augustine once tried to explain the difficulties he found in certain passages of Scripture. In commenting on verse four of *Psalm Eleven*, 'The eyes of God open and close upon humankind', he said: 'Sometimes when people find passages obscure it is as if God's eyes were closed, and so they are drawn to search more deeply. At other times they find God's eyes open and the passages of Scripture clear. Then they are enlightened and rejoice. But the existence of both obscure and clear passages in the sacred books are like the eyes of God which examine human beings and put them to the test. Let us not become bored and discouraged in God's sight but let us instead be energized when we read obscure texts. And when we understand a text we should not swell with pride but instead be strengthened'.[43] Saint Macarius expresses the wisdom of the monks when he writes: 'Be content with as much as you can understand and make an effort to put it into practice. Then whatever was hazy in your mind will be made clear to your spirit!'

Finally, reading Scriptures requires constant application. This is the single most necessary element if we are not to waste our time. Consistency helps us to harvest the Scriptures, to memorize them, and to interiorize the Word. The believer should read the Scriptures over and over until they penetrate his spirit and even his body. The ancient fathers recommended constant study and memorization of the scriptural texts, not just because they came from an oral culture, but because memorizing worked for them the way continual reading can work for us. The Word will come to life in us. So it is that the psalmist in Psalm 119 describes himself as murmuring the Scriptures, repeating the texts interiorly, reading the passages of Scripture again and again.

Father Pambo loved to say: 'The monks . . . speak with God without interruption and their lips are holy'.[44] The Scriptures were, in fact, both the voice of the desert fathers' prayers and the mirror for their contemplation. John Cassian pointed to consistency in reading the Scriptures specifically as an instrument for the growth of faith and the purification of interior prayer: 'Here is the goal you should strive for with all your strength: to apply yourself with constancy and concentration to reading the Scriptures, until continual meditation fills your mind and forms it somehow to its own likeness.[45]

Applying ourselves to *lectio divina* is a sign and a measure of our spiritual vitality. All spiritual progress results from reading and meditating on Scripture, in fact, and not from our independent will, which so often makes decisions in isolation from God's power.

Amos prophesied: 'The times are coming when I will send hunger on my people; not a hunger for bread nor a thirst for water, but a hunger to hear the Word of the Lord' (Am 8:11). Someone who is spiritual hungers and thirsts, and nothing can satisfy this desire except the Word. The monks of ancient times hungered and thirsted and there is plenty of evidence of their efforts at reading Scripture. Saint Jerome speaks of his hunger and of how his need to read the Scriptures was so intense that it kept him from sleeping. He counsels: 'Apply yourself night and day to reading the Scriptures. Sleep should overtake you while your book is in your hand, and the sacred page will welcome your nodding head like a pillow'.[46] Peter the Venerable praised the monk 'whose mouth repeats the holy words without ceasing'.[47]

The following citations from Psalm 119 refer to the performance of *lectio divina*: 'In the silence of the night I meditate on your word . . . ; in the middle of the night, I arise to read your word . . . ; your word is my comfort . . . ; I will meditate on your word . . . ; I desire your word. . . . ; your word gives me joy . . . ; night and day I meditate on your word'.

Constancy is essential really to knowing the world of the Bible, as Saint Jerome saw clearly: 'Reading invites application. Constant application produces familiarity. Familiarity produces faith and makes it grow'.[48] We cannot just pick and choose our moments with the Bible. It is necessary to immerse ourselves in it, to let it permeate our flesh, to grow so familiar with it that we possess it in the depths of our being and hold it in our memory. A good example of this is the *Magnificat*, the Song of Mary. It flows with biblical imagery, clearly the fruit of a heart that knew the Bible. We too need this constant familiarity with the Scriptures to pulse with their spirit, whether for a life of prayer or a life of faith-filled activity.

Those who frequent the Bible will become comfortable with the various kinds of books it contains, which reveal hidden things and mysteries to the reader. Only long and careful reading can make us familiar with the biblical language and forms of expression. Saint Isidore of Seville says: 'Anyone who wants to be united constantly to God should read the Scriptures frequently . . . and should willingly listen to them . . . , because all progress comes from reading them and meditating on them. Whatever we do not know we learn from our reading and whatever we've learned we store in our hearts by meditating'.[49] And Saint Ambrose advised: 'Meditate every day on the Word of God. Take Moses, Isaiah . . . , Peter, Paul, John, as your counselors. . . . Take Jesus Christ himself as your supreme model so that in this way you may approach the Father. Speak with these people; meditate with all of them all day long'.[50]

With these guidelines to help us, we can begin to read.

Read the text through and listen deeply to it. Stop immediately at the end. Pay attention to the text and try not to make use of your other faculties. 'In the reading itself,' says William Firmat, 'the Father, the Son and the Holy Spirit are present and speak in sweet conversation!'[51] Try to listen to the Word with an open spirit, even before you begin to reflect on it. Listen to the Word as it lives and speaks now. *Lectio divina* is done with your whole being: with your body, because normally you should pronounce the words with your lips; with your memory, which retains the words; with your intellect, which understands their meaning. The fruit of this reading is experience.

Read the text as it is, so that you may take its thoughts seriously in the form in which they are written. Do not be in too great a hurry to apply the text, or you may understand it only in the light of your own ideas or your particular circumstances. 'Subjectivism' is to be avoided at this point. Receive the Word in its objective meaning and understand it on its own terms.

Don't be eager for results, for some psychic sensation. To do so would be to reduce your reading to a mere technique and get you stuck once more in the world and its lures. Try not to have preconceived ideas about what will happen. This can lead you astray in a search for self-gratification. Do not let yourself go that way. This reading is not about introspection but about seeing our true selves as clearly as God sees us, as if from the point of view of another, from outside. Strive as much as possible to see with God's eyes, with that vision which you can begin to attain when you see and take in the world as God sees it and takes it in. Isn't Scripture exactly that—what God sees and takes in about the world and the human race?

Further, as you listen to God's Word, listen for God's voice in the *now*--as it always comes to us. True, we find this word tied to past events, to a history of times long past, but because it is the strength and power of God, it creates a new *today* for us every time we hear it. 'Today, hear God's voice!' (*Ps* 95.8)

It is less important to search for the meaning the Word had at the time it was written than to welcome it as if it were spoken today for the first time. Only in this way does it come to life and serve as a divine message for us, a source of creativity. Only in this way do we become aware that God is here, speaking to us today through Christ, and that we can listen to this voice, welcome it and absorb it. The seed is sown in good ground and it develops and grows, whether we wake or sleep (see *Mk* 4:26–27). The only effort we have to make is to remain in the Word. 'If you remain in my Word, you will truly be my disciples and you will know the truth' (*Jn* 8:31–32). To remain in the Word is to remain close to Christ and to become his disciple. The two disciples who were called in John 1:39 went with Christ and stayed with him. Jesus asked nothing more of them. 'If you remain in me and my words remain in you' (*Jn* 15:7), you will truly be able to pray and you will be heard. This is the essential thing in *lectio divina*: because at this point pure prayer flows from us, prayer which pleases God. In this prayer the purpose of *lectio divina* is accomplished.

Now let's take a look at all the richness we can find in this method of prayer.

In reading, it is also necessary *to search*, that is *to meditate*.

Search as you read! For whom or for what are we searching? Which of our faculties do we use, and what other means?

Searching means making an analysis of the text, giving attention to the words and their context. We certainly do not want to ignore the fact that today we can benefit from biblical scholarship, both literary and exegetical. When such learning is properly used it can enrich our reading. Saint Jerome was a perfect example of this in his day. We should therefore make use of the means our modern culture provides for arriving at a broader and deeper understanding of the text.

I don't mean by this that we should transform our *lectio divina* into a research project, but neither should we ignore any methods which will help us to better understand the text's meaning, which is the truly salvific aspect of Scripture. We might consider, for example, just how much it could help us to be aware of the literary form of various texts. The commentaries of the fathers or of spiritual writers, both ancient and modern, can be a real help in this task of searching the Scriptures. Yet even as we consult these learned sources, we must never forget—and here we run a constant risk—that the single purpose of *lectio divina* is to meditate on the text itself.

The understanding which *lectio divina* seeks in any text depends essentially on an understanding of the whole Bible—an understanding of the Bible by means of the Bible itself. We read the text and seek to understand it by using *concordances* or books which place parallel texts side by side. There are other books which shed light on the text as well. They draw out its message, affirm it and, under the guidance of the Holy Spirit, can provoke a comprehensive spiritual understanding. This way of praying over the Word may seem to be a passive or rather poor method, but it is actually *the method of the poor*, because it is available to anyone who is willing to put in the effort of reading the Bible again and again. The monks of ancient times lacked the scientific methods we have. They were often ignorant, even illiterate, but they memorized the Scriptures and knew them intimately. John Cassian describes their knowledge of the Bible as something lived and experienced: 'as our minds are renewed by this study, the very face of Scripture begins also to be renewed, and the beauty of this quite holy understanding is increased to the degree of our spiritual advancement'.[52] Blessed Francis of Siena was able 'to break the bread of God's Word with the people and to present it to them in an exhaustive way. His preparation was not studying theories but kneeling for a long time in adoration of Christ crucified'.[53] When asked about this, he answered with words which are a strong admonition for us: 'The teacher in *lectio divina* should be, not erudition but the Spirit's anointing, not knowledge but wisdom, not words on paper but love'.[54]

The purpose for which the Word of God was given to us, in fact, is spiritual anointing and love, not scholarship and science. And so, while we certainly should search the Scriptures with our intelligence and use all the means of scholarly analysis available to us, what really counts is our faith. Faith is meant to enlighten our intelligence. Faith is both the point of departure and the end point of our thinking. Faith is the only indispensable condition for encountering Christ in the text.

The most important part of our searching the Scriptures comes next: our reflection, our *rumination*, our chewing over the Word again and again. This term comes to us from the vocabulary of Saint Pachomius and is applied to the Word to indicate the operation by which we assimilate the Word we've read, heard and understood. It means to 'taste and see how good the Lord is!' (Ps 34:9).

William of Saint Thierry expresses it in this way: 'There is the same gulf between attentive study and mere reading as there is between friendship and acquaintance with a passing guest, between boon companionship and chance meeting.

Some part of our daily reading should be committed to memory each day, taken in, as it were, into the stomach to be more carefully digested and brought up again for frequent rumination, something that will take hold of the mind and save it from distraction.'[55]

If attention is the faculty we use most in reading, then memory is the most important faculty in rumination. Return again and again to the text. Rediscover its central theme and inscribe it deeply on your heart. Ruminating on the Word is like ingesting Scripture spiritually. Scripture becomes our food and drink through long hours of contemplation and reflection. This happens, John of Fécamp says, in *the mouth of the heart*, through *the palate of the heart*, and Guigo II specifies the first step of *meditation* as *chewing* over the text.

As we assimilate the text we have read and understood, we begin to enjoy its flavor. We begin to gather in the deep meaning of each turn of phrase. We hear in each individual text the echo of the whole of Scripture. Saint Pachomius' rule states: 'When the brothers are seated in their houses, they shall not engage in worldly speech, but if the housemaster has taught something from the Scripture, they shall reflect on it among themselves, relating what they have heard or what they can remember.'[56]

To remember Scripture and to keep it in our present awareness is not some mnemonic feat, because this we remember in the memory of the heart, which has stored up the words and images of the biblical text. *Lectio divina*, like the hebrew method of reading, not only happens in the mind but involves the whole human person: repeating the words aloud, focusing our attention, making a gift of ourselves through our senses, exercising our memories, until the words are imprinted on our hearts. Meditating is very active, as the Word itself indicates in Psalm 119: 'Be pleased, O Lord, with the words of my mouth and the murmuring of my heart.'

Rumination is the principal way in which the text becomes Word and lives anew in us. By this method, we become like wise scribes who can bring forth from the Scriptures treasures both old and new. Our murmurings echo the growl of the lion, which is the all-powerful Word of God. One of the most beautiful fruits of *rumination* is the memory it creates in us of God's deeds. The more our *rumination* springs from memory, the more our memory encompasses the whole mystery of salvation history in Christ. Our awareness itself becomes doxological.

Saint Basil is the person who best explained this *memoria Dei*: 'To have God as a firm foundation within oneself by means of the memory'[57] is for him the natural fruit of reading Scripture. This is true prayer, available to the most humble as well as to the most cultured of the brethren. Memory is always capable of bringing God to mind and so the memory itself is continually at prayer. 'The remembrance of God's marvelous works comes from reading', says Saint Basil, 'and holding the Scriptures in our memories is true meditation'.

Here, then, are a few fundamental thoughts about meditation.

After you do the *reading* itself, *ruminating* will introduce you to *meditating*. Meditating consists in making the Word of God so course through our life that it becomes an instrument for praying. To meditate is to acquire a taste for the Scriptures, not just a basic knowledge of them, or—to quote a medieval definition cited by the late Jean Leclercq—'to seek savor, not science. Scripture is Jacob's well, and by meditation we draw up from it the water which we then pour out in prayer'.[58] Meditating demands hard, constant work, but whole generations from the patristic age through medieval times have found riches in it. Even Saint Francis, who defined himself over against the monastic world, recommended this method and so it was preserved by the non-canonical mendicant orders.[59]

How do we meditate? The Bible gives no recipe, but it does offer a few suggestions.

One way of meditating is to find and then repeat a particular *theme* from different points of view. In Psalm 119, the theme is the Law. We find the same thing in Psalms 106 and 107, where the theme is the love God has shown for his people in history. In meditating as in journeying, the method is *repetition*.

Then there is the pauline type of meditation, a two-phase rhythm which moves *from a narrow to a broad focus*. In the first phase, the theme is focused quite specifically. In the Letters to the Galatians and to the Corinthians, for example, the crucifixion is applied personally. In the Letters to the Ephesians and the Colossians—the second phase—it is broadened and expanded to include the salvation of all persons.

There is a johannine method of meditation which we may call *cyclical*, in which the same themes are repeated again and again according to a catechetical plan.

There is also a *liturgical-ecclesiastical* method of meditation. We may celebrate an event in salvation history first from an ontological point of view, as when we recall the memory of the Nativity or the Resurrection, then in a soteriological light, as when we recall the memory of Epiphany or Pentecost. But there are also many other methods. What counts is that when we confront a text, we ask ourselves—as Mary did— what these words mean (Lk 1:29), and we store them up in our hearts so we can faithfully reflect on them (Lk 2:19). The Word of God will not do us violence. It is sweet. It is present more in the gentle breeze than in the great storm (cf. 1 K 19:12) and, like the Holy Spirit, it makes itself felt in an allusive, quiet way.

Guigo the Carthusian gives us a concrete example of meditation, and I enjoy sharing it because it very eloquently distinguishes what we are calling *meditation* from the meditation of scholasticism and the last few centuries. He begins his example with the gospel verse: 'Blessed are the pure in heart, for they shall see God' and he goes on to search for the kernel of this beatitude, purity of heart. Purity of heart does not lead Guigo to think about examining his conscience or regarding himself in the light of the gospel sayings. Instead, he turns to Psalm 24:3–4 and recalls the qualities used there to describe the person who enters into intimacy with the Lord. Then his recollection turns to Psalm 51:12: 'Create a clean heart in me, O God'. So, it is God who has the capacity to create a pure heart. It is God, not we, who can renew our spirits. We shall see God because of God's action in us. After searching hard for God, we shall at last see the face of the Lord by seeing God in the transfigured Christ. Life will purify us, death will refine us, and 'when we wake up again, we shall be satisfied with the vision of God' (Ps 17:15). That's how patristic meditation works!

Then Guigo interrupts his train of thought and says to his readers: 'Do you see how a little spark can ignite a tremendous fire?' There is a broadening which takes place in *lectio divina*, so that we are led to be more and more open to the Word of God. We fill our mouths to overflowing with God's words, and yet we still pant for more (Ps 119:131). The Scriptures are indeed a deep well, and the only means we have of drawing water from them is to meditate, to dialogue with the Spirit and with Christ, who presents himself through the biblical text as the Image of the Father.[60]

Theoleptus of Philadelphia has left these instructions on how to conduct our meditation: 'Read one page attentively, and penetrate its meaning. Do not be content with running quickly and superficially over the words, but listen to them with your full understanding and treasure their meaning for you. Then reflect on what you have read. Meditate and you will burn with fervor. In the same way that chewing your food lets you discover its various flavors, so repeating the divine words enlightens your intelligence and fills it with joy'.[61] In meditating we come to know the flavor of God's Word, and we develop an ever greater taste for it.

Isaac of Nineveh advises us: 'When we meditate, the words acquire a particular sweetness in our mouths, and we may repeat the same texts interminably without ever being satisfied'.

We may choose to stay with the same text and not move on to another. Why do we need another so long as we can still meditate more deeply on what we have, murmuring and repeating the same words to ourselves? When the Word of God speaks to us, God speaks to us. The Word urges us on and draws new things out of us, things that we never saw before. When we listen to the Word, we become 'someone who responds to the Creator'. It is here that we begin the next phase of *lectio divina*: prayer.

Praying is really the purpose, as well as the final goal, of *lectio divina*, but we need to exercise some discretion about it, because I think it is hard to discern this moment for someone else and to guide them through it. The moment of prayer is different for different people and it is more the result of *lectio divina* than part of it.

In a sense, everything we've been describing up to this point is already a form of prayer, but this is the point at which people who have been reading Scripture become aware that they have been praying all along and should feel it more than ever.

Meditating on our reading simply tends to produce in us a kind of rapture in God. Saint Augustine understood this and gave us the following advice: 'If the text is a prayer, pray. If it cries out, cry out. If it gives insight, rejoice. If it is a text which promises hope, hope. If it expresses fear, fear. The feelings you hear in the text are a mirror of your very self'.[62]

And so we enter into a conversation with God when we interiorize the feelings and the attitudes in the text, and then we cannot help but offer a prayer which is pleasing to God. The Word came to us and now it returns to God in the form of our prayer. 'When you listen, God speaks to you,' Saint Ambrose said, 'when you pray, you speak to God.' The movement between us and God is complete.

This is true christian prayer: prayer that can be described as supplication, petition, intercession, praise and thanks all at once, that is, prayer which knows the fullness of all those different moments and which takes place in relationship to the Other. At the same time, this prayer has been directed by Scripture and shaped by the Word of God and by the Spirit who was the origin of this Word and moving force of the Word's incarnation. Christian prayer is and always has been primarily *opus Dei*, the work of God. The Word, proclaimed, repeated, interiorized, meditated, sung, finally becomes contemplation—intercession directed toward the Father by Christ in the Holy Spirit. 'Try not to say anything without him', Saint Augustine continued, 'and he will not say anything without you'.[63] This means: pray with God's own words and then God will not have sent his Word to you in vain. The Word will have no secrets for you. It will say everything to you. God will show you everything.

William of Saint Thierry defines prayer as everything which springs from a heart touched by the divine Word. Prayer is truly the river that flows from the temple, in Ezekiel's image (Ez 47:1 ff). It flows from the temple where the Ark of the Covenant, the container of God's Word, is kept. Prayer flows from a heart which has been pierced by the two-edged sword, by the Word which penetrates and divides (Heb 4:12). This is where compunction is born. Prayer is my response to God, to God's self-gift to me in the reading. I give myself back to God in prayer. Saint Jerome speaks of 'talking with the Bridegroom in prayer', perceiving his presence as it emerges from the text and making it my own in loving colloquy. In the New Testament, in fact, the *anawim* respond to the Word of God, using the *Benedictus*, the *Magnificat* and the *Nunc Dimittis*—the same words which God's Word had already spoken to them in the books of the First Testament.

Prayer is a humble response offered by God's little ones, but in a way it also puts us on equal terms with God and enables us to respond with complete openness, because we are speaking to God with God's own words.

This is the type of prayer which flows from *lectio divina*: honest, direct, and powerful! There is no surer way for a Christian to arrive at authentic prayer. The Catholic Church understands and demonstrates this in the way it uses Scripture in the liturgy. The faithful respond to the proclamation of

Scripture readings with Scripture, with the acclamations of the Responsorial Psalm.

Oratio (prayer) necesssarily follows upon *lectio* and is specifically a response to reading Scripture. Prayer begins with song, with words of praise and thanks, 'How great you are, O Lord, my God', 'How great are your works, O Lord!' (Ps 104:1, 24); 'You make me glad, O Lord, by your actions, I am in awe of your works!' (Ps 92:5).

This is an intoxicating moment, which could easily result in tears of joy or in dance. I will dance before you, O Lord Most High! Here, we feel lost in the love of God. We want to summon our friends—the faithful, the believers, the poor—to share this experience, which is forever incommunicable (Ps 34:2 ff). Our hearts are so full of God that they cry out, 'The poor will see and be glad' (Ps 34:3), and we want everyone to taste and see how good and sweet the Lord is (cf. Ps 34:9).

Clearly, this intense feeling cannot last forever or be experienced every day, but when it is given to us, we should receive it with thankful hearts. We should never try to suppress it. David felt drunk with joy when he saw the Word of God carried before him in the Ark of the Covenant (2 Sm 6:14 ff). Hannah seemed tipsy when she spoke passionately to God (1 Sm 1:9–18). The prophets were often subject to these states of exalted joy and this is no special privilege of theirs. Often we share the same experience. We should not seek these moments as an end in themselves, of course, but when they are given, let us not waste them.

There then follows a phase of awe and amazement. The Word which has filled us with joy, the Word which was with God and is God now also dwells in our deepest selves and is our way, our light and our life. No longer do we need to cry out, we can simply allow this Word to drift, like incense, quietly and peacefully to heaven. This is the phase of the groaning of the Spirit, which we can neither understand nor express and of which we are sometimes barely even aware. What we should do is simply rest in the Word, and the Spirit will lift us up inwardly towards God, raise us up totally and carry us away. In these moments, *oratio* does nothing more than direct our faith and clarify it. Now we taste our faith, as Elijah tasted the bread prepared for his journey through the desert (1 K 19:5–8), as Hagar slaked her thirst in the desert (Gn 21:19), as John felt the physical presence of Jesus when he rested against his chest at the Last Supper (Jn 13:25).

We converse silently with God, with no other desire than to remain close. We are so near that we sense God's presence and we become ever more silent, like two lovers who, at a certain point after the excitement and happiness of conversation, simply take joy in being with each other. There is no more to say. They speak with their eyes and their hearts. In the same way, when we are this close, we know God's thoughts in our deepest being. We feel that we have discovered God's heart in the scriptural text, and we give ourselves to him.

Guigo II the Carthusian ended his *lectio divina* with this prayer: 'O Lord, when you break the bread of sacred Scripture for me, you reveal yourself. Grant, then, that the more I know you, the more I will want to know you, not from without, in the rind of the letter, but within, in the letter's hidden meaning. Nor do I ask this because of my own merits, Lord, but because of your merciful love. In my unworthiness, I confess my sins with the woman who said that even the dogs eat of the crumbs which fall from their master's table. Give me, Lord, a sign of what awaits me in the life to come. Give me a drop of water from that heavenly rain to refresh my thirst a little, because I am on fire with love for you.'[64]

All this is not easy. This prayer is a goal; it is not natural. That is why perseverance in prayer is necessary. We knock that the door may be opened. Or perhaps we should say that we must allow Christ to knock ever more loudly at the door of our hearts through the texts, until we are overcome by his voice and open the door from inside (cf. Rv 3:20).

Then he will come in and sit at table with us, and we will not even need to speak because when we are together with him we will not need words. He is the Word made flesh. We need do nothing but contemplate him in the final phase of *lectio divina*, which is contemplation.

We cannot arrive at contemplation through our own efforts. It is not a state which comes to us from outside ourselves. It is the natural fruit which has grown from the seed of praying the Word.

The Lord is always there, of course, with us at table. We knocked in prayer and we were brought to contemplation. The synergy we spoke of is at work here as well, because in the text he too has been knocking at our hearts, and he has been allowed into our deepest and innermost being. There is nothing more to do than to behold him and contemplate him like Mary of Bethany at the feet of the Master (Lk 10:39). And if we are distracted, his voice is always there to call us back. 'The Master is here and he is calling you' (Jn 11:28). Every page of Scripture reveals Christ to us and brings Christ out into our *lectio divina*. He makes himself present to us and calls forth in us amazement, surprise, and admiration. More than anything, contemplation is this experience. The loving gaze of God, which was revealed as focused upon us in *lectio divina*, has now become our own deepest interior vision, our way of seeing reality and other people, our way of discovering the presence of God everywhere. Contemplation is not the same as ecstasy. It is not an extraordinary experience. It is our ordinary way of seeing but it is now focused on the One who is 'the most beautiful child of the whole human race' (Ps 45:2), the One who 'is good and makes all things good' (Ps 103:3 ff and 119:68).

This is an experience of faith, not of visions. We continue to walk in the light of faith, not following apparitions (cf. 2 Cor 5:7). The veil which hung between us and the Scriptures has been removed because it has been dissolved in Christ (2 Cor 3:14). We are left with a contemplative consciousness. As Saint Paul describes in Ephesians 3:16–17: Christ lives in our hearts by faith. Our inward self, what we call our heart, contemplates him and sees him with the eyes of faith. So contemplation cannot be brought about by forcing our meditations to extremes or by any act of our own will. It is a pure gift from the One who gives light to our eyes and 'to the eyes of our hearts' (Eph 1:8).

We arrive at last at that consciousness of God for which the prophets prayed. Hosea 6:6 describes it this way: 'It is knowledge of God I want, not acts of the will (burnt sacrifices)'. John of Fécamp described his experience as follows: 'My spirit enjoys nothing so much as that moment in which I raise up to you alone, my God, the simple gaze of a pure heart. Then everything is still, everything is calm. My heart burns with love. My soul overflows with joy. My memory is strong and my understanding enlightened. And my inward spirit is aflame with the desire to behold your beauty, to be carried away in love for all that is real but invisible'.[65]

Contemplation should bring us to love the God we cannot see, as the Christmas preface puts it, in the words of Saint Paul (2 Cor 4:18). We are carried away in a love that is tied more to faith than to our sentiments or our emotions. We sense that God takes us without our taking any particular created thing from God. We give ourselves over completely. Let us not forget what leads us along this passage from prayer to contemplation: faith united with love, the faith which lets us behold the glory of God shining in the face of Christ (2 Cor 4:6), the love which frees us from all our thoughts and ideas and fills us instead with desire and longing.

Meditation ends and contemplation begins when we can renounce all our busy thinking. Anthony Bloom proposed this principle: 'Once meditation has brought us to contemplation, it becomes useless to seek or to think. It becomes foolish to think about God when one stands before God, in God's presence. The fathers always warn us against this tendency to substitute thoughts about God for the encounter with God'.[66]

There is little left to say. Only individually can we discover the dimensions of contemplation, the height, the depth, the length and the breadth of the mystery of Christ (cf. Eph 3:18).

When we arrive at this point, we are no longer even aware of praying; our prayer has become perfect. Saint Anthony the Great, the father of monasticism, used to say wisely: 'Prayer is not yet perfect so long as the monk is conscious of himself and his praying!' No longer should we be able to turn our gaze back on ourselves or feel ourselves praying; we should be aware only of the face of Christ and in his light be able to contemplate the light of God the Father. Our body is present but it no longer weighs us down and, without our noticing, it is transformed from glory to glory into the image of the One we contemplate (2 Cor 3:18). It is as if we discover ourselves in the act of beholding the glory of Christ, and we become one with him. *Lectio divina*, when it has reached the threshold of the vision of God in this way, becomes eschatological. It prepares for that final moment of Christ's coming, when contemplation will become everlasting. *Lectio divina* provides a foretaste of our final and ultimate fulfillment. It brings a bit of it into the present, and in this sense it is prophetic.

It would be pointless for me to remind believers who are already making great efforts to apply themselves to the Word that all that remains is for them to make it real in their lives. I would love to begin another section here with a few directives. I could include a whole array of methods for *lectio divina*, and call this section: 'Make the Word real in your lives, and you will give witness for the Lord'.

But that is not part of the theme of this book, and besides, I want to leave space for the Word to exercise its own power: calling, converting and working in those who hear it. For those who hear, the Word will become real (Mt 7:4; Jn 1:22). Only in this way will they be able to reach the goal they had in mind when they began *lectio divina*, closeness and communion with God. The measure of this communion with God—which Jesus described in the language of the human relationships of brothers, sisters, children—is whether one does the will of God. Do our actions, at all times and in all circumstances, embody the Word (Mt 12:48–50)?

Caesarius of Arles warned that hearing the Word can never leave the hearer the same. God's Word either redeems or condemns the person who hears it, as does the Body of Christ in the Eucharist (cf. 1 Cor 11:29). He used to preach: 'If one does not consume the Word of God by putting it into practice, like manna, it will produce worms which will eat it'. This is the judgement the Word, the two-edged sword, carries with it.

Once the Word has been proclaimed and we have accepted it, storing it up and reflecting upon it in our hearts, as Mary did the word of the *annunciation* (Lk 1:38; 2:19, 51), then we must imitate Mary in her *visitation*, putting ourselves at the service of others (cf. Lk 1:39–45). Really hearing the Word should lead to *praxis*: going out into the world and touching human hearts, trying to speak to them a word that recognizes that Image of God they carry within, that prototype, that model, which is always receptive to the Creator's voice. We should be putting ourselves to the task of making the Word so concrete that people will be able to give glory to the Father, who with the Word produces in us both good will and good actions (cf. Phil 2:13).

Lectio divina is not a school of prayer unless it is a school for living. In this school, God speaks to us, calls us, and draws out our response, but only to send us forth, to make us apostles, 'those who are sent', missionaries to the world.

This step forward from *lectio divina* to *praxis* was summed up by Saint Ambrose: '*Lectio divina* guides us into doing good works. Just as the goal of meditating on words is to memorize them and we recall the words we meditated on, so the goal of meditating on God's word is action.'

CONCLUSION

With these few elementary notes on *lectio divina*, we hope to have provided readers with an opportunity to renew or to develop a taste for a way of reading Scripture which is as old as the Church itself, and which has deep roots in Judaism.

I don't think we've said anything new. We've simply made a quick review of the patristic and monastic traditions, which made *lectio divina* a form of daily nourishment within the context of praying the *opus Dei,* the Liturgy of the Word.

Let me conclude with this observation: I am convinced that the believer who follows this method, adapting it to his own personality and spirit, is like an iconographer, like those painters of divine images who live on Mount Athos and even nearer home. To write an icon is to make a visible *lectio divina,* to translate the Word into an image. In a text, as in a painting, the face of Christ emerges little by little, filled with the light and beauty that we see in contemplation.

In God's light we see light (cf. Ps 36:10). Saint Augustine says that: 'God speaks many things to the heart, but in hidden ways. When he speaks with a loud voice and cries out "I am your salvation!", a great echo is produced in the deep silence of the heart.' May *lectio divina* help us to hear God's voice every day, crying out in us: 'I, the Lord, am your salvation' (Ps 35:3).

Notes

[22] On these jewish origins and on the practice of the Church Fathers, see the section 'Lectio Divina et lecture spirituelle' in the *Dictionnaire de la Spiritualité,* volume 9:column 470ff; see further P. Lenhardt and A. C. Avril, *La lettura ebraica della Scrittura* (Bose 1989).

[23] See Jean Leclercq, *The Love of Learning and the Desire for God,* (New York 1961) pp 72, 153–155. In 'Lectio Divina from the Eleventh to the Fourteenth Centuries' (*Studia Monastica* 8 [1956] 267–293), Leclercq has clearly shown the resistance the monastic world put up against this new scholastic culture, but he has also pointed out that 'in the overwhelming majority of the texts we have, the monks show a kind of consistency in their idea of what a human life is, first of all, then in their idea of the Christian life and finally in their idea of a specifically monastic life. Their vision of life and of human behavior is integrated with their vision of the economy of salvation'. Thus, it is not just a question of different methods of reading Scripture, but of the monks' very vision of a life which should spring out of the *lectio divina.* This vision has been subsequently treated more

deeply by François Vandenbroucke and, more recently, by G. R. Evans, who has shown how, using as a base the format *lectio-disputatio-praedicatio*, Bernard, both a biblical 'exegete' and someone who knew how to apply the 'technique', subordinated all his work to a single aim: 'to render each one who reads or listens to the Word of God able to welcome the divine illumination into his spirit'. ('Lectio, disputatio, praedicatio: St. Bernard the Exegete', in *Studia Monastica* 24 [1982] 127–145, especially 143–145).

24 See, for example, Guy de Valous, *Le monachisme clunisien des origines au XVème siècle*, (Paris 1970) 327ff. The *lectio* is still mentioned and practised, but the accent is on the liturgy of the psalms. As a consequence, so-called 'spiritual reading' develops. See, in this regard, the section 'Lectio divina et lecture spirituelle', cited above (note 22), as well as the observations of J. A. Vinel: 'Spiritual reading is not the same as the practice of *lectio divina* . . . , its focus is different from that more ancient way of reading: in spiritual reading, it is nearly at the point of prayer that one seeks to be permitted union with God, the reading just serves as a sort of trampoline, as an instrument to edify the soul, to nourish it or to help it to recollect itself. In the Middle Ages, on the other hand, one can always find the expression *lectio divina*, meaning a way of drawing near to Scripture with an attitude that harmonizes it with daily life, and above all, the reading is itself more immediately oriented toward the experience of God'. ('La lectio divina' in *Vie Consacrée* 54 [1982] 289–290).

25 The Second Vatican Council, *Constitution On Divine Revelation*, 'Dei Verbum' 25

26 See Guigo II's Letter to his friend Gervase (*The Ladder of Monks*), below, pages 100–114. Guigo's work is neither the first nor the only one of its kind in the Middle Ages, but, with its four steps, it has the advantage of systematizing the subject with great clarity. The idea of uniting prayer with reading runs through the entire tradition from Origen to Jerome, and the triple formula, *lectio, meditatio, oratio* is the one mainly used in the Middle Ages, above all by the Cistercians. One point remains absolutely the same in all these gradations, a point on which J. A. Vinel quite rightly insists: 'These three or four attitudes are always steps in a single journey. . . . They are united among themselves by a common bond so intimate that at times it seems that even the terms being used to describe them are being used equivocally, one taking the place of the other. But the ancient spirituality systematized meditation and prayer to the point of demanding a determined sequence of thoughts or feelings with an established order of precedence.' Guigo himself distinguishes the four levels 'making clear that he is not compartmentalizing four static states but describing a single dynamism in which these levels intersect and mutually influence each other . . . It is true that *lectio* provokes different attitudes and behaviors, but we cannot discern among them any logical sequence or—much less— a rigid division. *Lectio* unifies the different phases of its essential approach along the lines of its own deepest objective: union with God'. (Vinel [see above, note 24] 290–291). This is already perhaps less true in Hugh of Saint Victor's early tract *De meditatione*: the intellectual tone and the interest in moral life present in this work tend to isolate the stage of meditation and give it its own validity, though it occurs within a ladder of five steps: *lectio-meditatio-oratio-operatio-contemplatio*. The object of *meditatio* is no longer simply the Scripture (Part II), but also 'creation' (Part I) and finally 'morality' (Part III).

[27] Guigo, *Letter to Gervase* 3; below, p. 100.

[28] Symeon the New Theologian, *Oratio* 15: *De sacris Scripturis* (PG 120:385C) 'Other writings, truly, can be penetrated and understood by whoever reads them, but the writings which are divine and speak of salvation can neither be understood nor treasured without the enlightenment of the Holy Spirit'.

[29] Gregory the Great, *In Ezechielem Homelia* 7 11 (PL 76:846AB).

[30] William of Saint Thierry, *Epistola ad fratres de monte Dei* 121 (SCh 223:239); *The Golden Epistle*, translated Theodore Berkeley (Kalamazoo 1971) p. 51.

[31] P. Y. Emery, 'La méditation de l'Ecriture', in Fr. François and Fr. Pierre-Yves, *Méditation de l'Ecriture et Prière des Psaumes* (Bellefontaine 1975) 17.

[32] Saint Augustine, *Ennar in Ps.* 85.6 (PL 37:1085).

[33] Saint Ambrose, *In Psalmum 118 Expositio* 68 (PL 15:1270B): '*Tota intendat in verbo*' (This is the version given in the edition of L. F . Pizzolato, *Commento al Salmo CXVIII/I* [Milan-Rome 1987] 246. An alternate reading: is '*in verbum*'.) Ambrose continues: 'And behold, from the very start it would seem to her that she was hearing the voice of Him whom she still did not see, and with deep perception she would recognize the fragrance of his divinity. Those who have a living faith often have this kind of sensation'.

[34] Caesarius of Arles, *Sermo* 782 (CCSL 103:324).

[35] Saint Augustine, *De Trinitate* 152.2 (PL 42:1057f).

[36] William of Saint Thierry, *Epistola ad fratres de monte Dei* 120 (SCh 223:239); *The Golden Epistle*, p. 51.

[37] Saint Jerome, *Epistola ad Eustochium* 22.25 (PL 22:411); translated by Joan M. Petersen in *Handmaids of the Lord* (Kalamazoo 1996) 190.

[38] William of Saint Thierry, *Super Cantica canticorum* 128 (SCh 82: 109); translated by M. Columba Hart, *Exposition on the Song of Songs* (Spencer/Kalamazoo 1970) 23.

[39] Saint Peter Damian, *Vita Sancti Romualdi* 31 (PL 144: 982f)

[40] Saint Gregory the Great, *In Ezechielem Hom* 1.10.11 (PL 76: 889AB).

[41] Saint Jerome, *In Ezechielem Comm* 12 (PL 25:369D).

[42] *Non enim verba ad te quaerit Deus, sed cor*: Saint Augustine, *Enarr in Ps.* 134.11 (PL 37:1746).

[43] Saint Augustine, *Enarr in Ps.* 10.8 (PL 36:136).

[44] *Apophthegmata patrum*, alphabetic series, Pambo 7; L. Mortari, *Vita e detti dei Padri del deserto* 2 (Rome 1971) 135–136; English translation by Benedicta Ward SLG, *The Sayings of the Desert Fathers* (Kalamazoo 1975) 197.

[45] John Cassian, *Conlationes* 14.10 (PL 49:970B; CSEL 13:410). For an English translation, see *John Cassian: The Conferences*, translated by Boniface Ramsey OP. Ancient Christian Writers 57 (New York 1997).

[46] Saint Jerome, *Epistola ad Eustochium* 22.17 (PL 22:404); *Handmaids*, 182.

[47] Peter the Venerable, *De miraculis* 120 (PL 189:887A).

[48] Saint Jerome, *Epistola ad Asellam* 45.2 (PL 22:481).

[49] Isidore of Seville, *Sententiae* 3.8.2–3 (PL 83:679B).

[50] Saint Ambrose, *In Psalmum 118 Expositio* 137 (PL 15:1382C). The context provides a very concrete image which helps to clarify Saint Ambrose's thinking: 'Reflect all day long on the Law: a cursory reading will not suffice for you. If you go out to buy a field or to purchase a house, you bring with you someone who is a little more knowledgeable about the law; you pay close attention to its stipulations, and to be sure that you won't fall into some error, you rely on someone else's expertise. Well now you are engaged in trying to get ownership of your very self. Bargain aggressively about your price! Take a good look at all that you are, at the name you bear, at what profit it all brings you. This is no field, no coin, no precious gemstone, but Jesus Christ who is beyond any price, beyond any magnificence!' For more on this comment of Saint Ambrose, Cf. D. Gorce 'L'usage de la Sainte Ecriture d'après l'*Expositio in psalmum 118* de Saint Amboise' in *La Vie Spirituelle* 8 (1923) 616–641.

[51] William Firmat, 'Esortazione', in *Analecta Monastica*, second series = Studia Anselmiana 31 (Rome 1953) 43, lines 397–404.

[52] John Cassian, *Conlationes* 14.11.1 (PL 49:972B; CSEL 13:411).

[53] 'The Legend of Blessed Francis of Siena', in *Monumenta Ordinis Servorum S Mariae* 5 (Brussels) 26. Publication was begun in 1897 and suspended in 1930.

[54] *Ibid.*

[55] William of Saint Thierry, *Epistola ad fratres de monte Dei* 121–122 (SCh 223:239–241); *The Golden Epistle*, pp 51–55.

[56] Saint Jerome's text of Pachomius' *Praecepta* 122 The pachomian text is 'Sitting in their houses, they shall not speak . . . but they shall reflect on the words spoken by the housemaster'. See Armand Veilleux, trans., *Pachomian Chronicles and Rules (Kalamazoo 1981)* = Pachomian Koinonia 2:164. The Jerome text, in translation, appears in the same volume, page 191. On meditation on the Scriptures as a fundamental element of Pachomius' spirituality, see L. Cremaschi, *Pachomio e discepoli: regole et scritti* (Bose 1988) 89.

[57] Saint Basil, Letter 2.4 (PG 32:230B).

[58] Arnold of Bohières, *Speculum monachorum* 1 (PL 184:1175), addressed to a monk still in the novitiate, cited by Jean Leclercq, *The Love of Learning and the Desire for God* (New York 1961, 1974) 90.

[59] See U. Occhialini, 'Francesco di Assisi', in *Pregare la Bibbia nella vita religiose* (Bose 1983) 238–268.

[60] Guigo, Letter to Gervase 6, below, p. 100 (*The Ladder of Monks*, pp. 69–73).

[61] Extract from 'Analyse de la prière'; see *La prière*, Cahiers de la Pierre-qui-Vire (1954) 159–160 Theoleptus was Metropolitan of Philadelphia, c. 1250–c. 1326.

[62] See Saint Augustine, *Enarr in Ps.* 29.16 (PL 36:224).

[63] Augustine, *Ennar in Ps.* 85.1 (PL 37:1082): *Noli aliquid dicere sine illo, et non dicit aliquid sine te.*

[64] Guigo, *Letter to Gervase* 6, below, p. 100 (*The Ladder of Monks*, 73).

[65] See Jean Leclercq, *Un maître de la vie spirituelle au XIème siècle, Jean de Fécamp* (Paris 1946) 142.

[66] Anthony Bloom, 'Prière et sainteté', quoted from typewritten work

in the possession of the author. See Anthony Bloom, 'Prayer and Holiness' in *God and Man* (London -Crestwood, New York 1983) 73–120. See also Louis Bouyer, *Introduction to Spirituality* (London-Collegeville 1961) 55: 'When our *lectio divina* is worthy of its name, contemplation does not come as a kind of superstructure, as if from without. Contemplation is, even if obscurely, the prime mover of this *lectio* with regard to our faith, and its crown with regard to the love nourished by that faith.'

GUIDELINES FOR
LECTIO DIVINA

6

CALL ON THE HOLY SPIRIT

Before you begin to read Scripture, *pray* to the Holy Spirit to come upon you, so that 'the eyes of your heart may be opened' and God's face may be revealed to you, not in a physical vision but by faith. Pray with confidence that you are being heard, because God will always give the Holy Spirit to those who ask humbly and openly. If you wish, you may use these words:

> Our God, Father of light, you have sent your Son into the world, the Word made flesh, to reveal yourself to your human children: Send your Holy Spirit upon me now, so that I may encounter Jesus Christ in the Word which comes from you. May I come to know him and to love him more intensely, and so come to the happiness of your kingdom. Amen.

7

OPEN THE BIBLE AND READ

You have the Bible in front of you. This is not just any book but the book that contains God's Word. God wants to speak to you today, person to person, by means of this book.

Read the text over a few times, slowly, paying attention. You can read a passage from the lectionary or directly from one of the books of the Bible, but read calmly; try to *listen to* it with your whole heart, with your whole understanding, with your whole being. Silence both outside and inside will help you to concentrate on what you are reading and to listen to it.

8

SEARCH BY MEDITATING

Reflect on the text with your understanding, enlightened by God's own light. As you proceed, you may want to make use of some aids. Helpful instruments are: concordances, exegetical commentaries, commentaries from the Church Fathers or other spiritual writers. These can help you understand the deeper and fuller meaning of 'the written words'. Pray that your intelligence and your ability to reason may be receptive to God's will and to God's message for you. Don't forget that all the books in the Bible form a whole, and so you should *interpret scripture with scripture.* Always seek out Christ, crucified and risen, who is the focus of every page throughout the Bible. The Law, the prophets and the apostles all speak of him. *Reread* the text and you will eventually see that the message evokes certain responses deep within you. *Chew the words over* in your heart and apply the message to yourself, to your life situation, but avoid getting lost in yourself by psychologisms or an examination of conscience. Let yourself be passive and let the Word draw you forth by its attractiveness. Focus on Christ. Reflect on Christ who dwells in you and not just on yourself alone. It is he who will transform you.

9

PRAY TO THE LORD WHO HAS SPOKEN TO YOU

Now that you have been filled with the Word of God, *speak* to your Lord. Better yet, *respond* to him: to his invitations, to his inspirations, to his calls, to his messages and to the directions that he has given you in his Word, as you have understood it by the light of the Holy Spirit.

Pray with frank honesty and trust. Pray without ceasing and do not get tripped up by too many human words. These are moments of *praise*, of *thanksgiving*, of *intercession*. Get your attention off yourself and follow the attraction you feel toward the face of the Lord. You have come to know that face in Christ. Walk in his footsteps without looking back. Free up your creativity, which will drive you outward, and your sensitivity, feelings and emotions. Put all that you are at the service of the Word, in obedience to the God who has spoken to you.

10

CONTEMPLATE . . .
CONTEMPLATE. . . .

You are now in partnership with the Lord. Try to see everything through his eyes: yourself, other people, life events, history, every creature, and the whole world. *Contemplation is seeing everything and everyone through God's eyes.* When you can see and evaluate everything from God's point of view, you will feel God's peace. Above all, you will experience what is called *divine macrothymía*: the feeling and the consciousness of the whole. All things are grace, and the whole universe is an epiphany of God's love.

This is the moment when the Word visits your soul. It is indescribable, ineffable, experienced by many yet unique to each person.

The Lord puts into your heart some block against thinking. You find that you cannot meditate on his Word in any logical fashion. God grants you instead a kind of burning participation in the divine life, a communion of love with God. This is beyond anything that can be described in words, even beyond silence itself.

11

KEEP THE WORD IN YOUR HEART

Store up in your heart the Word you have received, as did Mary, the woman who was a perfect listener. *Store it up, care for it, call it to mind.* At various times of the day, go over the passage—even just one verse from it—in your memory. This fosters *awareness* of God, which can unify and center your whole day: your work, your rest, your social life and your moments of solitude. When the Word which has been planted in you like a seed seems inert, wake it up! Give it your attention until it becomes your companion throughout the day.

12

DON'T FORGET THAT TO LISTEN MEANS TO OBEY

If you have really listened to the Word, you will put it into practice; you will act creatively to bring about among the people in your world all that God has shown you. *To listen is to obey.* You should make some practical resolutions which are based on your state in life and your position in society, always allowing the Word to be the guiding force in your life.

Commit yourself to putting God's word into action, so you will not be condemned by the One who will judge us. Judgement will be based not on how much we have heard, but on how well we have put what we have heard into practice in our lives—in the personal, social, professional, political and ecclesiastical dimensions of our lives. After we listen, the task left to us is to believe and to let our faith bear *the fruit of the spirit:* 'love, joy, peace, patience, good will, kindness, faithfulness, humility, self-control' (Gal 5:22). Thus we will come to experience the great joy of God's merciful love.

TWO LETTERS ON
LECTIO DIVINA

13

A Letter From Father Enzo, Prior of Bose, to Brother John

Dearest John,

In the course of the liturgy you celebrate daily with your brothers and sisters in community or at least every Sunday in church, you hear Scripture readings and listen to a homily, a gift which explains and concretizes the texts which were read. In this way you stand before the Word of God, living and active and echoing within you. You stand before the very presence of the Lord, before Christ the Sower who is sowing the seed of his Word in you.

In the liturgy, the table is set with two kinds of food: Word and Eucharist are given to you for your journey, for your exodus from this world to the Father. They will nourish you and prevent you from getting weak as a member of God's people. Here you are given a taste of the pilgrim's bread and a taste for the One who feeds you, consoles you, keeps you strong and protects you from illness.

But since the liturgy is the central experience of the christian life, you will also want to renew it privately during the course of each day, in the solitude of your room. Or perhaps you will want to share this renewal with your brothers and sisters in community, those companions and guides God has given you.

You can be sure that you will not be able to understand and assimilate the Scriptures by relying on yourself alone and on your own scanty resources. There are certain conditions for a fruitful reading of Scripture, in which the Word of God brings about in you what you cannot bring about in yourself. These are just the preliminaries which allow your reading to be permeated with the spirit of faith in Christ, to be filled with the gifts of the Holy Spirit, and to lead you to a contemplative vision of God the Father.

By reading in the Spirit, I mean *praying* the Bible, *lectio divina*.

1. LECTIO DIVINA IN THE EXPERIENCE OF ISRAEL AND OF THE CHURCH

In the First Covenant, ancient Israel prayed the Word and used the Word to pray. You can see these communal practices described in chapter 8 of Nehemiah. This method of explaining and praying the Word is the forerunner of *lectio*. It became the classic jewish model of prayer and Christianity inherited it (cf. 2 Tm 3:14–16). The New Testament doesn't describe this method so much as make reference to it in several passages.

Generations of Christians continued praying this way, rarely falling into any form of non-biblical piety or using any prayer that did not recognize the absolute primacy of the Word in the Church's life of prayer. All the Church Fathers, in both East and West, practised this method of *lectio divina* and encouraged the faithful to do the same in their homes. As a result, they have left us their wonderful commentaries on Scripture, the fruit of their *lectio*.

And how can we skip over the monastic tradition? The monks made *lectio divina* the center of their lives both in the desert and in their communities. They called it the *ascesis of the monk* and his daily bread, for they knew that 'human beings cannot live by bread alone but by every word which comes from the mouth of God' (Dt 8:3 and Mt 4:4). At a certain point, they found it necessary to set this method down in writing to help the novices, who wanted to learn to take the Word into themselves through the Spirit who not only sanctifies but even divinizes them.

Origen proposed *theía an á gnosis* to the jewish rabbinic school. Saint Jerome punctuated his reading of Scripture with prayer. John Cassian gave an example of *meditation*. The Carthusian Guigo II called *lectio divina* the monks' 'Stairway to Paradise'. Saint Bernard of Clairvaux extolled Scripture as honey on the heart's palate. William of Saint Thierry, in his *Golden Epistle* and many other works, outlined the method of *lectio divina* and tried to encourage all Christians to pursue it as *the golden way* to dialogue and to the ineffable colloquy with God.

This method nourished the faith of whole generations right through the 1300s, and even then Saint Francis of Assisi practised it regularly. But in the High Middle Ages, the scholastic method began to turn *lectio divina* into lectures on Scripture by introducing the *quaestio* and the *disputatio*. During the centuries when *lectio* as prayer was eclipsed, the way was opened to the more psychological and introspective methods of the *devotio moderna* and the ignatian forms of meditation. *Lectio divina* was preserved as a method only in monasteries and among the Servants of Mary. But it was there, waiting to reappear when the Second Vatican Council recommended it in *Dei Verbum* 25: 'There is a need for all to keep in constant contact with Scripture, using *lectio divina* . . . , the method of careful *meditation*, and let all remember that the reading of Scripture should be accompanied by *prayer*.'

Surely it was the Holy Spirit who willed that this way of listening to the Word and praying over it should not be lost over the centuries.

2. CHOOSING A PLACE FOR LECTIO DIVINA

When you want to immerse yourself in this *prayerful reading*, your first job is to select *a place where you can be quiet and alone*, where you can pray to your Father in secret (Mt 6:5–6) and maybe even reach contemplation.

Your own private room can be a place where you taste the presence of God and maintain your awareness of God. This place is also, in fact, the arena for your heart's struggle. It is the desert where Jesus prayed and was tempted (Mk 1:1, 35; Mt 4:1–11). It is the place where God draws you close to speak to your heart and to fill you with divine gifts, transforming the arid chasms of your heart into lush valleys and doorways of hope (Hos 2:15). Then, in this solitary place you will find your spiritual youth renewed, you will find your own song to sing tor your Lord, your Bridegroom. You will sense how much you belong to him alone and how you can live in peace with all persons and all creation (cf. Hos 2:18–25).

Your own room can be a sanctuary where God puts you to the test by the Word and humbles you. But as he does so, he educates, consoles, and nourishes you. You will surely feel the presence of the adversary, who will tempt you to turn away from being alone, who will make you feel the loneliness, who will distract you with nagging thoughts, who will try to lead you astray with myriad practical concerns. Don't lose heart. Don't give up. Instead, take on this demon in hand-to-hand combat, for the Lord is never far away and God will not just stand there to see how well you're fighting but will actually struggle for you and in you. If it is helpful, make use of an icon, a cross, a lighted candle, or a prayer stool. Never hesitate to use these things, but don't fall for fads and passing trends. Use them to remind you that you are not just studying the Bible or just reading words. You are praying: you are standing before God, ready to listen to God, ready to converse with God.

If the temptation to quit comes over you, resist it, even if it means sitting in silence and feeling nothing. Resist the temptation to give up if you want to meet God in personal prayer, because it takes time to become used to solitude and silence, and to detach from the whirlwind of things on your mind and the company of your friends.

3. A TIME OF SILENCE FOR GOD TO SPEAK

For your *lectio divina* try to choose a time of day and a place which will provide you with some external silence. This is the necessary condition for interior silence.

The Master is here and he is calling you (Jn 11:28), and to hear his voice you must silence other voices. To listen to the Word you must lower the volume of other words. There are some times of the day which are more likely to provide silence than others: the middle of the night, early in the morning, in the evening. You must consider your own daily work schedule, but whatever time you choose, make the choice once and stay faithful to it. You are not taking your prayer seriously if you go out to meet the Lord whenever there's an idle moment between tasks. Prayer isn't a filler for your empty moments. The Lord cannot be pigeon-holed. And don't even think of saying: 'I don't have time!' This excuse makes you an idolater. You have twenty-four hours at your disposal each and every day. If you get enslaved by your schedule, then that schedule is the god you worship!

Learn to make times of silence for yourself and let *lectio* create a rhythm in your day and in your life. You know that we are called to pray always, without growing weary (Lk 18:1–8; 1 Tm 5:17), but you also know that when we do this at specific times explicitly and visibly, *the awareness of God* will begin to sustain our whole day. Are you in love with God? Are you reaching out towards God? Well then, do not balk at consecrating to God a little of your time every day, just as you set time aside daily for your wife or your husband, your relatives or your friends.

And don't forget to make the time you set aside for *lectio* adequate for this task. Don't try for a quick fix. You need time to calm down, to come to peace. A few minutes are not enough. For good *lectio*, according to the Fathers, you need at least an hour.

We hear so many words every day; we read so many! We have to be careful not to drown the Word with our own words. There is no end to talk in the world. It's everywhere. How can the Word speak in all this din? Doing *lectio divina* at a regular time every day gives you the opportunity to evaluate the world's words in the light of God's Word. The world speaks to us constantly, and both the quantity and quality of the world's words can scramble the sound of God's voice until it bears no fruit in us from day to day (cf. Mk 4:13–20). What sense does it make to read everything we can get our hands on, to feed ourselves on all the world's issues, to stuff ourselves with things that leave the heart divided and unfocused and then to pretend that we are living by the Word which comes from the mouth of God? We have to exercise some prudence and make some choices between words and the Word, or else we will end up as nothing but dilettantes, hearers who become paralyzed when our path leads us up against any real challenge.

4. A LARGE, GOOD HEART

God calls you to the silent solitude in which the two of you can converse in prayer. God wants *to speak to your heart*.

The Bible speaks of the heart as the center of the human person, the deepest and most authentic part of us, and as the seat of our faculty of understanding. And so, *the principal organ* used in *lectio divina* is the heart, because it is the nucleus in which each human person exists as a unique, unrepeatable mystery. Yet you have read of an uncircumcised heart (Dt 30:6; Rom 2:29), a heart of stone (Ez 11:19), a divided heart (Ps 119:13 and Jer 32:29), and a blind heart (Lam 3:65). All these expressions indicate a heart that is far from God, that has not been touched by faith. A believer's heart can become weighed down with dissipation and drunkenness and the concerns of this life (Lk 21:34). It can become sick, hardened and so blocked up that it can no longer recognize or understand the Lord's words and actions (Mk 6:52 and 8:17). It can become unstable, inconstant, and tend to lose or forget the Word (2 Pt 3:16; Lk 8:13). A heart can begin to draw its nourishment from what is merely human, from the latest ideologies or even from its own pride, which is the worst sin. So when you are getting ready to spend time listening to God, take your heart in your hands and raise it up toward God, so that God may make it a heart of flesh: whole, steady and cleansed. Only when your heart becomes like that of a little child can it receive God's gifts (Mk 10:15).

Only when the Lord has made your heart new can it be open and ready to listen. The Lord has promised to give a new heart to anyone who asks (Ez 18:31), to soften and mold our hearts until they fit the Word. But before we will raise them up, we must be convinced in the first place that these hearts of ours are hardened (Ps 119:36). Every day God cries out to us: 'If only you would listen to my voice! Harden not your hearts!' (Ps 95:8; Heb 3:7). The hardened heart claims that it is God's Word which is hard. Even believers do this: 'This is a hard word; who can accept it?' (Jn 6:60). Ask God to give you *a big heart, a heart that can hear (leb shomea')*, as Solomon the wise once did (1 K 3:5).

When you sit down to do *lectio divina*, remember the parable in which the Lord is pictured as a sower in the act of sowing the Word. You are one of the four types of soil: either rocky, or a footpath open to everything that passes, or a patch of thorns, or good, rich soil. The Word must find this good, rich soil in you; then *'when you have heard the Word with a good, whole* heart, (en kardía kalê kaì agathê), you will keep it and produce fruit by faithful perseverance' (Lk 8:15).

When someone whose heart has been purified, focused and made whole celebrates *lectio divina*, the Father, Son, and Holy Spirit will come and make their dwelling place with that single-hearted person (Jn 14:23 and 15:4).

The human heart was made for the Word and the Word for the heart. The lyrics of Psalm 119:111 describe this marriage, in which God's Word becomes your own and your heart sings out the joy of belonging to God.

This is the heart of a disciple, a heart so receptive to God's intentions that it can experience the Word *with little or no explanation*, a heart truly seated at Christ's feet and ready to listen like Mary of Bethany (Lk 10:39), a heart capable of storing the biblical words and reflecting on them as Mary the Mother of Jesus did (Lk 2:19 and 51). This kind of heart can be yours.

'Lift up your hearts!' the liturgy cries out at the beginning of the Eucharist. *'Lift up your hearts!'* is also the invitation call to *lectio divina*.

5. CALL UPON THE HOLY SPIRIT

Take the Bible in your hands and hold it in front of you with the same reverence you would give to the Body of Christ. Make an *epiclesis*, an invocation of the Holy Spirit. The Spirit directs the Word's activity. The Spirit caused the Word to speak and write through the prophets and those who composed the wisdom literature, through Jesus, the apostles, and the evangelists. The Spirit gave the Word to the Church so that eventually it could find its way, whole and entire, to you.

The Word spoken by the power of the Holy Spirit is comprehensible only by the Spirit's guidance (*Dei Verbum* 12). Arrange everything in your life to open the way for the Spirit to come to you—*Veni Creator Spiritus: Come, Holy Spirit!*—in its full force, its *dynamis*, and to remove the veil from your eyes so that you may see the Lord (Ps 119:18; 2 Cor 3:12–16). The Spirit gives life! Only the letter kills! This is the same Spirit that came to Mary, overshadowing her with power and generating in her the *Logos*, the Word made flesh (Lk 1:34). This is the Spirit that came upon the apostles, bringing them to the fullness of truth (Jn 16:13). This Spirit will do the same for you: it will generate the Word in you and lead you to the fullness of truth. *What we sometimes call 'spiritual reading'*—lectio divina—*means reading in the Holy Spirit and with the Holy Spirit those things that were dictated by the Holy Spirit.*

Wait for the Spirit's coming, even though it seems to tarry (Hab 2:3). Find secure hope in Jesus' words: 'If you, who are bad, know how to give your children good things, how much more will the Father give the Holy Spirit to those who ask him' (Lk 11:13).

You will hear his powerful Word within you: *'Ephphatha*: Be opened!' (Mk 7:34). Then you will feel no longer alone, but in good company as you stand before the biblical text, like the Ethiopian who was reading Isaiah but did not understand it until Philip arrived and by the text brought into his silent heart the voice of the Holy Spirit he had received on Pentecost (Acts 8:26–38), or like the disciples themselves, who needed the Risen Lord to open their minds to the understanding of the Scriptures (Lk 24:45).

Without an epiclesis, lectio divina *remains just a human effort, an intellectual activity.* We could say that in it we 'learn knowledge' but not 'divine Wisdom'. Reading on one's own like this, without discerning the Body of Christ in the Scriptures, is reading condemnation to ourselves (cf. 1 Cor 11.29).

So pray however you can, in whatever way the Lord enables you; or use these words for your prayer.

> Our God, Father of light, you sent your Word, the Wisdom which comes from your mouth, into the world, that she might have dominion over all the peoples of the earth (Si 24:6–8). You willed that she make her dwelling place in Israel and that she make known your will through Moses, the prophets, and the psalmists (Lk 24:44), and speak to your people about the Messiah—Jesus—who was to come. Finally, you willed that he who is your only Son, that same Word and Wisdom eternally with you, become flesh and, conceived by the power of the Holy Spirit and born of the Virgin Mary (Lk 1:35), pitch his tent among us (Jn 1:1–14).
>
> Send upon me the Holy Spirit, that I may have a heart capable of listening (1 K 3:5). May your Spirit stand before me in these holy Scriptures and generate the Word in me.

May your Spirit take away the veil from my eyes (2 Cor 3:12–16), lead me to the fullness of truth (Jn 16:13) and give me understanding and faithfulness.

I ask all this through Jesus Christ, our Lord, who is blessed forever and ever. Amen!

Above all, you can use Psalm 119 as an aid in this preparatory prayer, for it speaks about listening to the Word. This psalm has special meaning for *lectio divina*. It speaks between the dialogue of the Lover and the Beloved, the believer and the Lord!

6. READ!

Now open the Bible and read the text. Never open it at random. The Word of God deserves to be eaten whole, not nibbled at casually. Follow the cycle of readings in the lectionary with an open mind, accepting whatever passage the Church offers you. Or else read a book of the Bible from beginning to end, in a *sequential reading*, a *lectio cursiva*.

Following either the lectionary or the sequence of a biblical book is essential if a faithful, daily reading of texts is to have continuity. This will also help you avoid falling into a subjectivism which chooses only the passages which you like or which merely fill your emotional needs. This is an iron principle to which you must remain faithful.

You may choose a book or one of the readings from the daily lectionary because the Church recommends it for a particular liturgical season. Do not jump around from text to text: *one passage, one episode, a few small verses are more than enough!* And if you do your *lectio* based on the Sunday readings, remember that the first reading (the First Testament) and the third reading (the Gospel) are parallels and you will benefit from praying over both together. The lectionary for feasts is a great gift, put together by people who are very spiritually astute. The daily lectionary is unfortunately more fragmented. If this causes you difficulty, it will be better for you to do a *sequential reading* of a single biblical book.

Read the text more than once. Read it many times and even out loud. If you have some knowledge of the original languages, Hebrew or Greek, read that version. Otherwise be content with a good translation.

Always try to use the Septuagint and Vulgate versions, if your educational level is up to it. These are favored translations, which the Church has venerated over the centuries.

If the passage you wish to pray over is so familiar to you that it repeats itself in your memory automatically or too fast, don't be afraid to resort to methods which will slow you down and help you to get beneath the surface connections. Write the text out. Make several copies! A friend of mine, a monk who is also an exegete of international repute, once told me in confidence that when he does *lectio divina*, he recopies the text again and again to see what differences may exist between what is *in his memory* and what is *actually written*. Don't read only with your eyes, but by careful attention try to print the text on your heart.

Also read the parallel passages indicated by the marginal notes. These are a great help, especially if you are using the Jerusalem Bible. Broaden the passage, stretch it by placing other passages which deal with the same message alongside the reading of the day. Remember, the Word interprets itself. *'Scripture is the interpreter of Scripture'*. This is the great rabbinic and patristic criterion for *lectio divina*.

Let your reading become listening (audire), and let your listening become obeying (oboedire). Slow down! It is necessary *to relax (vacare) with the readings*, because they are made to be listened to. *Then the Word will make itself heard!* In the beginning was the Word, not the Book, as in Islam! God speaks in *lectio*. Our reading is our means of listening to God. 'Hear, O Israel!'—this is God's constant call. It resounds in the text and echoes from the text out towards you.

7. MEDITATE!

What does it mean, to meditate? This is not always easy to say. Certainly, it means *to deepen the message you have read and to find out what God wants to communicate to you.* You must do some work, make some effort at attentive and deep reflection on the reading. In times past, when many Christians could learn the Scriptures only by memorizing them, reflection was actually made easier by repeating the words in their hearts. You too must dedicate yourself to reflecting on the readings, using contemporary methods in proportion to your intellectual gifts and education.

Although it is always true that we learn 'not by book-learning but by the Spirit's presence, not knowledge, but insight, not just words on paper but love (*non eruditione sed anuniatione, non scientia sed conscientia, non carto sed caritate*), this is not a slogan which justifies undisciplined or sporadic reading, or reading which ignores the rigors of serious biblical research and the many modern aids we have to help us understand the texts. Why not turn to the commentaries of the Church Fathers on the various books of Scripture? There are many good translations of them. A concordance is also a great help in the task of commenting on Scripture with Scripture. There are also modern exegetical studies and spiritual commentaries. You can evaluate the relative quality of many of these works for yourself. Some of them merely pretend to be serious spirituality, while in reality they contain nothing but personal opinions or eccentric interpretations which square with neither the texts nor tradition. Above all, avoid commentaries which advertise themselves as 'new applications of the Word', but really exploit the Word for their own purposes. Exercise some caution even with the spiritual commentaries you find in both the ferial and the festive lectionaries. Sometimes these interpretations of the texts are a little forced and reflect the personality and words of the writers more than they do the Word of God.

'Listening is not just passively receiving a given text. It also consists in the believer's effort to penetrate the text, to get to the bottom of the divine Word and find its unequivocal meaning. It is related to working diligently and tenaciously to apply the Word to one's life', says Origen.

All these exegetical, patristic and spiritual commentaries are certainly useful tools for *meditation* and for our personal growth in understanding. Yet *in lectio divina what is important is that our effort be personal. It need not necessarily be private.* All effort is more fruitful within the daily, lived experience of a community, a brotherhood or sisterhood, for it is in relationship to others that one truly becomes a disciple of the Word. In community, the Word *is not just read together but lived and experienced together.*

Personal effort will search out the spiritual point of the text. This is not the same as getting hooked on the phrase that inspires the greatest feelings of personal guilt. The central message is always best synchronized with the mystery of the Lord's death and resurrection. Work at getting at that spiritual sense, the sense which is consistent in Scripture, the spiritual sense which is basic to both the Fathers and modern exegetes. In commenting on Scripture with Scripture, you can seek what the Lord is saying to you.

Don't expect to find only what you already know. What complacency! Don't expect necessarily to find something to please you or ease some situation in your life. This is giving in to subjectivism. *Not all texts are completely understandable right away!* Try a little humility and recognize that so far you've understood little or even nothing at all, and you'll come to a greater understanding later on. This is another form of obedience: if you admit that you still need to be milk-fed, you won't expect to be nibbling on solid food (cf. 1 Cor 3:2; Heb 5:12).

When you get to the point of understanding a little of it, chew over the words in your heart (the *rumination* recommended by the Fathers). Then apply them to yourself and to your life-situation, without getting lost in psychologism or introspection, and without getting locked into an examination of conscience. God is speaking to you. Think about God, not about yourself! Don't let yourself get paralyzed by a scrupulous analysis of your own shortcomings and limitations while the divine Word is demanding your attention.

The Word will discern the state of your heart, judge you and convict you of sin, but remember that God is greater than your conscience (cf. 1 Jn 3:20). When God wounds your heart this way, he always does it with truth and mercy.

Instead of thinking about yourself, stand in awe of the One who is speaking to your heart and of the food which is being offered to you—sometimes a lot, sometimes a little, but always good nourishment. Be amazed that you are welcoming the Word into your heart here and now, without having to travel to the heavens or beyond the seas to find it (cf. Dt 30:11–14). Let yourself be drawn by the Word and transformed into the image of the Son of God, without your even knowing how. The Word which you have received is your life, your joy, your peace and your salvation. God is speaking to you. You need to listen in amazement. Like the Hebrews who witnessed the great works of the Exodus, and like Mary who sang: 'God has done great things in me, holy is his name' (Lk 1:49), you too should be marveling! God is revealing himself to you. The face of your Beloved, the unspeakable Name of God. Open your heart in welcome! This is the time for faith! God is teaching you directly to model your life on the life of the Son. God is giving himself to you in the Word. Welcome God as you would embrace and hold the infant Christ. God is giving you a holy kiss, being wed to you as Lover and Beloved. Let your heart celebrate the One who is Love, stronger than death, stronger than *sheol*, stronger than your sins. God is giving birth to you as *logos*, as word, as child. Meditation, rumination should lead you to this: to become a dwelling-place for the Father, the Son, and the Holy Spirit.

Your heart is a sanctuary. Your whole person is a temple. This is the theandric reality: the mystery of the divine in the human.

8. PRAY!

Now speak to God. Respond to God's invitations: to the calls, the inspirations, the messages God has given you by the Holy Spirit's power in the Word. Do you see that you have been welcomed into the very heart of the Trinity, into the eternal conversation among Father, Son, and Spirit? Why stop at being an onlooker? Enter the conversation and speak as a friend speaks to a friend (Dt 34:10). You need not attempt any longer to conform your thoughts to God's. Instead, simply seek God's presence. *Meditation* was only for the sake of this *moment of prayer*. Now you've arrived! Don't engage in spiritual gossip with God, but instead speak with openness and confidence and without fear. Don't be self-conscious. Rather, be wholly conscious of the face of God which shines forth from the text as Christ, the Lord. Free up your creative impulses: your sensitivities, feelings and emotions, and direct them into this relationship with the Lord. I cannot give you directions here, because each person is unique and knows best how to meet his or her God. Besides, one can't even speak satisfactorily about this experience for oneself, much less for another. What can one say about the fire when one is immersed in it? What can one say about the prayer of contemplation which comes at the end of *lectio divina* except to say that it is a glowing log which never burns out and that it inflames the believer's heart with love for the Lord?

The art of experiencing the Indescribable, the divine Presence! *Lectio divina* wants to lead you there, where you can contemplate God as God's own beloved, where you can repeat the words of God's own beloved in joy, in wonder and in self-forgetfulness. This path is not always easy and straight. Don't think that you can just run along its way. Passionate love alternates with fear, gratitude with a complete absence of feeling, enthusiasm with bodily weariness, words which speak with words which are mute, God's silence with your silence: all these experiences are present and serve as the stock in trade of your *lectio divina*, day after day.

What is important is staying faithful to our daily encounter with the Lord. Sooner or later the Word will open a passageway into our hearts and clear away all the obstacles we set up, obstacles which are always present in any journey of faith and prayer. Only the person who is faithful to the Word knows God's faithfulness: that God will never fail to be available and to speak to our hearts. The faithful person knows that there are times when the Word of God seems absent (1 S 3:1), but that these times are followed by an epiphany. The Word will shine forth. The faithful person knows that these difficult, uncomfortable, dry times are a grace insofar as they remind us of the distance between our experience of God and God as God is.

Thank God for the gift of the Word and for the people who proclaim and explain it to you. Intercede for all your sisters and brothers as the text calls them to your mind, with all their virtues and failings. Try to unite being fed with the Word with your Eucharistic food.

Store up what you have seen, heard and tasted in *lectio*. Go over it in your heart and in your memory *as you go along in the company of others*, and seek humbly to share with them the peace and blessing you've received. You will also find a way to bring God's Word into social, political and professional situations; the daily reality of life.

God needs you as an instrument in the world to help create new heavens and a new earth—a future day which awaits you when, in dying, you will see God face to face. Then you will see how you have been and still are *a living letter* written by Christ, a *lectio divina* for your sisters and brothers, and how you really are the very Son of God.

Yours,

Enzo

A Letter from Guigo II,
Prior of the Grand Chartreuse
to his friend Gervase

1. GREETING

BROTHER GUIGO, to his dear brother Gervase: rejoice in the Lord. I owe you a debt of love, brother, because you began to love me first; and since in your previous letter you have invited me to write to you, I feel bound to reply. So I decided to send you my thoughts on the spiritual exercises proper to cloistered monks, so that you who have come to know more about these matters by your experience than I have by theorizing about them may pass judgment on my thoughts and amend them. And it is fitting that I should offer these first results of our work together to you before anyone else, so that you may gather the first fruits of the young tree which by praiseworthy stealth you extracted from the bondage of Pharaoh, where it was tended alone, and set it in its place among the ordered rows, once you had grafted on to the stock like a good nurseryman the branch skillfully cut from the wild olive.

2. THE FOUR RUNGS OF THE LADDER

One day when I was busy working with my hands I began to think about our spiritual work, and all at once four stages in spiritual exercise came into my mind: reading, meditation, prayer and contemplation. These make a ladder for monks by which they are lifted up from earth to heaven. It has few rungs, yet its length is immense and wonderful, for its lower end rests upon the earth, but its top pierces the clouds and touches heavenly secrets. Just as its rungs or degrees have different names and numbers, they differ also in order and quality; and if anyone inquires carefully into their properties and functions, what each one does in relation to us, the differences between them and their order of importance, he will consider whatever trouble and care he may spend on this little and easy in comparison with the help and consolation which he gains.

Reading is the careful study of the Scriptures, concentrating all one's powers on it. Meditation is the busy application of the mind to seek with the help of one's own reason for knowledge of hidden truth. Prayer is the heart's devoted turning to God to drive away evil and obtain what is good. Contemplation is when the mind is in some sort lifted up to God and held above itself, so that it tastes the joys of everlasting sweetness. Now that we have described the four degrees, we must see what their functions are in relation to us.

3. THE FUNCTIONS OF THESE DEGREES

Reading seeks for the sweetness of a blessed life, meditation perceives it, prayer asks for it, contemplation tastes it. Reading, so to speak, puts food whole into the mouth, meditation chews it and breaks it up, prayer extracts its flavor, contemplation is the sweetness itself which gladdens and refreshes. Reading works on the outside, meditation on the pith: prayer asks for what we long for, contemplation gives us delight in the sweetness which we have found. To make this clearer, let us take one of many possible examples.

4. THE FUNCTION OF READING

I hear the words: 'Blessed are the pure in heart, for they shall see God'. This is a short text of Scripture, but it is of great sweetness, like a grape that is put into the mouth filled with many senses to feed the soul. When the soul has carefully examined it, it says to itself, 'There may be something good here. I shall return to my heart and try to understand and find this purity, for this is indeed a precious and desirable thing. Those who have it are called blessed. It has for its reward the vision of God which is eternal life, and it is praised in so many places in sacred Scripture.' So, wishing to have a fuller understanding of this, the soul begins to bite and chew upon this grape, as though putting it in a wine press, while it stirs up its power of reasoning to ask what this precious purity may be and how it may be had.

5. THE FUNCTION OF MEDITATION

When meditation busily applies itself to this work, it does not remain on the outside, is not detained by unimportant things, climbs higher, goes to the heart of the matter, examines each point thoroughly. It takes careful note that the text does not say: 'Blessed are the pure in body', but 'the pure in heart', for it is not enough to have hands clean from evil deeds, unless our minds are cleansed from impure thoughts. We have the authority of the prophet for this, when he says: 'Who shall climb the mountain of the Lord, and who shall stand in his holy place? He whose hands are guiltless and whose heart is pure.' And meditation perceives how greatly that same prophet seeks for this purity of heart when he prays: 'Create a pure heart in me, O God', and in another place: 'If I know that there is wickedness in my heart, the Lord will not hear me'. It thinks what care the saintly man Job took to preserve this purity when he said: 'I have made a pact with my eyes, so that I would not think about any maid.' See how this holy man guarded himself, who shut his eyes lest he should look upon vain things, lest he should perhaps unguardedly see that which afterward he should long for despite himself.

After meditation has so pondered upon purity of heart, it begins to think of the reward, of how glorious and joyful it would be to see the face of the Lord so greatly longed for, 'fairer than all the sons of men', no longer rejected and wretched, not with that earthly beauty with which his mother clothed him, but wearing the robe of immortality and crowned with the diadem which his Father bestowed upon him on the day of his resurrection and glory, 'the day which the Lord has made'. It thinks how this vision will bring it the fullness of which the prophet says: 'I shall be filled when your glory appears'. Do you see how much juice has come from one little grape, how great a fire has been kindled from a spark, how this small piece of metal, 'Blessed are the pure in heart, for they shall see God', has acquired a new dimension by being hammered out on the anvil of meditation? And even more might be drawn from it at the hands of someone truly expert. I feel that 'the well is deep', but I am still an ignorant beginner, and it is only with difficulty that I have found something in which to draw up these few drops. When the soul is set alight by this kindling, and when its flames are fanned by these desires, it receives a first intimation of the sweetness, not yet by tasting but through its sense of smell, when the alabaster box is broken; and from this it deduces how sweet it would be to know by experience the purity that meditation has shown to be so full of joy.

But what is it to do? It is consumed with longing, yet it can find no means of its own to have what it longs for; and the more it searches the more it thirsts. As long as it is meditating, so long is it suffering, because it does not feel that sweetness which, as meditation shows, belongs to purity of heart, but which it does not give. A man will not experience this sweetness while reading or meditating 'unless it happened to be given him from above'. The good and the wicked alike can read and meditate; and even pagan philosophers by the use of reason discovered the highest and truest good. But 'although they knew God, they did not glorify him as God', and trusting in their own powers they said: 'Let us sing our own praises, our words are our own.' They had not the grace to understand what they had the ability to see. 'They perished in their own ideas', and 'all their wisdom was swallowed up', that wisdom to which the study of human learning had led them, not the Spirit of wisdom who alone grants true wisdom, that sweet-tasting knowledge that rejoices and refreshes the soul in which it dwells with a sweetness beyond telling. Of this wisdom it is said: 'Wisdom will not enter a disaffected soul.' This wisdom comes only from God; and just as the Lord entrusted the office of baptizing to many, but reserved to himself alone the power and the authority truly to remit sins in baptism, so that John called him by his office and defined it when he said: 'This is he who baptizes', so we may say of him:'This is he who gives the sweetness of wisdom and makes knowledge sweet to the soul. He gives words to many, but to few that wisdom of the soul which the Lord apportions to whom he pleases and when he pleases.'

6. THE FUNCTION OF PRAYER

So the soul, seeing that it cannot attain itself to that sweetness of knowing and feeling for which it longs, and that the more 'the heart abases itself', the more 'God is exalted', humbles itself and betakes itself to prayer, saying: Lord, you are not seen except by the pure of heart. I seek by reading and meditating what is true purity of heart and how it may be had, so that with its help I may know you, if only a little. Lord, for long have I meditated in my heart, seeking to see your face. It is the sight of you, Lord, that I have sought; and all the while in my meditation the fire of longing, the desire to know you more fully, has increased. When you break for me the bread of sacred Scripture, you have shown yourself to me in that breaking of bread, and the more I see you, the more I long to see you, no more from without, in the rind of the letter, but within, in the letter's hidden meaning. Nor do I ask this, Lord, because of my own merits, but because of your mercy. I too in my unworthiness confess my sins with the woman who said that 'even the little dogs eat of the fragments that fall from the table of their masters'. So give me, Lord, some pledge of what I hope to inherit, at least one drop of heavenly rain with which to refresh my thirst, for I am on fire with love.

7. THE EFFECTS OF CONTEMPLATION

So the soul by such burning words inflames its own desire, makes known its state, and by such spells it seeks to call its Spouse. But the Lord, whose eyes are upon the just and whose ears can catch not only the words, but the very meaning, of their prayers, does not wait until the longing soul has said all its say, but breaks in upon the middle of its prayer, runs to meet it in all haste, sprinkled with sweet heavenly dew, anointed with the most precious perfumes, and he restores the weary soul, he slakes its thirst, he feeds its hunger, he makes the soul forget all earthly things: by making it die to itself. He gives it new life in a wonderful way, and by making it drunk he brings it back to its true senses. And just as in the performance of some bodily functions the soul is so conquered by carnal desire that it loses all use of the reason, and man becomes as it were wholly carnal, so on the contrary in this exalted contemplation all carnal motives are so conquered and drawn out of the soul that in no way is the flesh opposed to the spirit, and man becomes, as it were, wholly spiritual.

8. SIGNS OF THE COMING OF GRACE

But, Lord, how are we to know when you do this, what will be the sign of your coming? Can it be that the heralds and witnesses of this consolation and joy are sighs and tears? If it is so, then the word consolation is being used in a completely new sense, the reverse of its ordinary connotation. What has consolation in common with sighs, joy with tears, if indeed these are to be called the tears and not rather an abundance of spiritual dew, poured out from above and overflowing, an outward purification as a sign of inward cleansing. For just as in the baptism of infants by the outward washing, the inward cleansing is typified and shown, here conversely an outward washing proceeds from the inner cleansing. These are blessed tears, by which our inward stains are cleansed, by which the fires of our sins are put out. 'Blessed are they who weep' so, 'for they shall rejoice.' When you weep like this, my soul, recognize your spouse, embrace him for whom you long, make yourself drunk with this torrent of delight, and suck the honey and milk of consolation from the breast. The wonderful reward and comforts which your spouse has brought and awarded you are sobbings and tears. These tears are the generous draught which he gives you to drink. Let these tears be your bread by day and by night, the bread which strengthens the human heart, sweeter than honey and the honeycomb. O Lord Jesus, if these tears, provoked by thinking of you and longing for you, are so sweet, how sweet will be the joy which we shall have in seeing you face to face? If it is so sweet to weep for you, how sweet will it be to rejoice in you? But why do we give this public utterance to what should be said in secret? Why do we try to express in everyday language affections that no language can describe? Those who have not known such things do not understand them, for they could learn more clearly of them only from the book of experience where God's grace itself is the teacher. Otherwise it is of no use for the reader to search in earthly books: there is little sweetness in the study of the literal sense, unless there be a commentary, which is found in the heart, to reveal the inward sense.

9. HOW GRACE IS HIDDEN

O my soul, we have talked like this too long. Yet it would have been good for us to be here, to look with Peter and with John upon the glory of the Spouse and to remain awhile with him, had it been his will that we should make here not two, not three tabernacles, but one in which we might all dwell and be filled with joy. But now, the spouse says, 'Let me go, for now the dawn is coming up', now you have received the light of grace and the visitation which you asked for. So he gives his blessing, and withers the nerve of the thigh, and changes Jacob's name to Israel, and then for a little while he withdraws, this Spouse waited for so long, so soon gone again. He goes, it is true, for this visitation ends, and with it the sweetness of contemplation; but yet he stays, for he directs us, he gives us grace, he joins us to himself.

10. HOW, WHEN GRACE IS HIDDEN FOR A TIME, IT WORKS IN US FOR GOOD

But do not fear, bride of the Spouse, do not despair, do not think yourself despised, if for a little while he turns away his face from you. These things work together for your good, and you profit from his coming and from his withdrawal. He comes to you, and then he goes away again. He comes for your consolation, he goes away to put you on your guard, for fear that too much consolation should puff you up, and that, having the Spouse with you always, you should begin to despise your brothers and to attribute this consolation, not to his grace, but to your natural powers. For this grace the Spouse bestows when he pleases and to whom he pleases; it is not possessed as though by lawful title. There is a common saying that too much familiarity breeds contempt. And so he withdraws himself, so that he is not despised for being too attentive, so that when he is absent he may be desired the more, that being desired he may be sought more eagerly, that having been sought for he may at last be found with greater thankfulness.

Then, too, if we never lacked this consolation, which is a mere shadow and fraction in comparison with the future glory that will be shown in us, we might think that we have here on earth our eternal home, and so we should seek the less for our life in eternity. So, therefore, lest we should consider this present exile our true home, this pledge our whole reward, the Spouse comes and withdraws by turn, now bringing us consolation, now exchanging all this for weakness. For a short time he allows us to taste how sweet he is, and before our taste is satisfied he withdraws; and it is in this way, by flying above us with wings outspread, that he encourages us to fly, and he says in effect: See now, you have had a little taste of how sweet and delightful I am, but if you wish to have your fill of this sweetness, hasten after me, drawn by my sweet-smelling perfumes, lift up your heart to where I am at the right hand of God the Father. There you will see me not darkly in a mirror but face to face, and 'Your heart's joy will be complete and no one shall take this joy away from you'.

11. HOW MUCH THE SOUL MUST BE ON ITS GUARD AFTER IT HAS BEEN VISITED BY GRACE

But take care, bride of the Spouse. When he goes away, he does not go far; and even if you cannot see him, you are always in his sight. He is full of eyes in front and behind, you cannot hide from him anywhere, for he surrounds you with those messengers of his, spirits who serve to bring back shrewd reports, to watch how you behave when he is not there, to accuse you to him if they detect in you any marks of wantonness and vileness. This is a jealous spouse. He will leave you at once and give his favors to others if you play him false with anyone, trying to please anyone more than him. This Spouse is fastidious, he is of gentle birth, he is rich; 'He is fairer than all the children of men,' and so he will not deign to take a bride who is not fair. If he sees in you any blemish, any wrinkle, he will at once turn away from you. He cannot bear uncleanness of any kind. So be chaste, be truly modest and meek, if you wish often to enjoy your Spouse's company.

I am afraid that I have talked too long of this to you, but I have been compelled to it by the abundance and the sweetness of my material. I have not deliberately drawn it out, but its very sweetness has drawn it out of me against my will.

12. REVIEW

Let us now gather together by way of summary what we have already said at length, so that we may have a better view by looking at it altogether. You can see, from what has already been said by way of examples, how these degrees are joined to each other. One precedes another, not only in the order of time but also of causality. Reading comes first, and is, as it were, the foundation; it provides the subject matter we must use for meditation. Meditation considers more carefully what is to be sought after; it digs, as it were, for treasure which it finds and reveals, but since it is not in meditation's power to seize upon the treasure, it directs us to prayer. Prayer lifts itself up to God with all its strength, and begs for the treasure it longs for, which is the sweetness of contemplation. Contemplation when it comes rewards the labors of the other three; it inebriates the thirsting soul with the dew of heavenly sweetness. Reading is an exercise of the outward senses; meditation is concerned with the inward understanding; prayer is concerned with desire; contemplation outstrips every faculty. The first degree is proper to beginners, the second to proficients, the third to devotees, the fourth to the blessed.

13. HOW THESE DEGREES ARE LINKED TO ONE ANOTHER

At the same time these degrees are so linked together, each one working also for the others, that the first degrees are of little or no use without the last, while the last can never, or hardly ever, be won without the first. For what is the use of spending one's time in continuous reading, turning the pages of the lives and sayings of holy men, unless we can extract nourishment from them by chewing and digesting this food so that its strength can pass into our inmost heart? It is only thus that we can from their example carefully consider our state of soul, and reflect in our own deeds the lives about which we read so eagerly. But how is it possible to think properly, and to avoid meditating upon false and idle topics, overstepping the bounds laid down by our holy fathers, unless we are first directed in these matters by what we read or what we hear? Listening is a kind of reading, and that is why we are accustomed to say that we have read not only those books which we have read to ourselves or aloud to others but those also which our teachers have read to us.

Again, what use is it to anyone if he sees in his meditation what is to be done, unless the help of prayer and the grace of God enable him to achieve it? For 'every gift and every perfect gift is from above, coming down from the Father of lights'. We can do nothing without him. It is he who achieves our works in us, and yet not entirely without us. 'For we are God's fellow workers', as the apostle says. It is God's will, then, that we pray to him, his will that when his grace comes and knocks at our door, we should willingly open our hearts to him and give him our consent.

It was this consent that he demanded from the Samaritan woman when he said: 'Call your husband.' It was as if he said: 'I want to fill you with grace, and you must exercise your free choice.' He demanded prayer from her: 'If you only knew the gift of God, and who he is who says to you, Give me drink, you would perhaps ask him for living waters.' When the woman heard this, it was as if the Lord had read it to her, and she meditated on this instruction in her heart, thinking that it would be good and useful for her to have this water. Fired with the desire for it, she had recourse to prayer, saying: 'Lord, give me this water, that I may thirst no more'. You can see that it was because she had heard the Lord's word and then had meditated on it that she was moved to prayer. How could she have pressed her petition, had she not first been fired by meditation? What profit would her meditation have been, if the prayer that followed had not asked for what she had been shown she should desire? From this we learn that if meditation is to be fruitful, it must be followed by devoted prayer, and the sweetness of contemplation may be called the effect of prayer.

14. SOME CONCLUSIONS

From this we may gather that reading without meditation is sterile, meditation without reading is liable to error, prayer without meditation is lukewarm, meditation without prayer is unfruitful, prayer when it is fervent wins contemplation, but to obtain it without prayer would be rare, even miraculous. However, there is no limit to God's power and his merciful love surpasses all his other works; and sometimes he creates sons for Abraham from the stones themselves, when he forces the hard-hearted and reluctant to comply of their own free will. He acts like a prodigal father or, as the proverb has it, he takes the ox by the horn, when he enters where he has not been invited, when he dwells in the soul that has not sought him. Although we are told that this has occasionally happened to Saint Paul, for instance, and certain others, we ought not to presume that it will, for this would be like tempting God. Rather we should do our part, which is to read and meditate on the law of God, and pray to him to help our weakness and to look kindly on our infirmities. He teaches us to do this when he says: 'Ask and you will receive, seek and you will find, knock and the door will be opened to you.' For then 'the kingdom of heaven submits to force and the forceful take it by storm'.

From these definitions you can see how the various qualities of these degrees are linked one with another, and the effects which each one produces in us. Blessed is the man whose heart is not possessed by any other concern and whose desire is always to keep his feet upon this ladder. He has sold all his possessions, and has bought the field in which lies hid the longed-for treasure. He wants to be free from all else, and to see how sweet the Lord is. The man who has worked in this first degree, who has pondered well in the second, who has known devotion in the third, who has been raised above himself in the fourth, goes from strength to strength by this ascent on which his whole heart was set, until at last he can see the God of gods in Sion. Blessed is the man to whom it is given to remain, if only for a short time, in this highest degree. In truth he can say: 'Now indeed I experience God's grace, now with Peter and John upon the mountain I gaze upon his glory, now with Jacob I delight in the embraces of the lovely Rachel.'

But let such a man beware lest after this contemplation, in which he was lifted up to the very heavens, he plunged violently into the depths, and after such great graces turn again to the sinful pleasures of the world and the delights of the flesh. Since, however, the eye of the human heart has not the power to bear for long the shining of the true light, let the soul descend gently and in due order to one or other of the three degrees by means of which it made its ascent. Let it rest now in one, now in another, as the circumstances of time and place suggest to its free choice, even though, as it seems to me, the soul is the nearer to God the farther it climbs from the first degree. Such, alas, is the frailty and wretchedness of human nature!

In this way, then, we see clearly by reason and the testimony of the Scriptures that the perfection of the blessed life is contained in these four degrees, and that the spiritual man ought to occupy himself in them continually. But is there anyone who holds to this way of life? 'Tell us who he is and we will praise him.' There are many who desire it, but few who achieve it. Would that we were among these few!

15. FOUR OBSTACLES TO THESE DEGREES

There are commonly four obstacles to these three degrees: unavoidable necessity, the good works of the active life, human frailty, worldly follies. The first can be excused, the second endured, the third invites compassion, the fourth blame. Blame truly, for it would be better for the man who for love of the world turns his back on the goal if he had never known God's grace, rather than, having known it, to retrace his steps. For what excuse will he find for his sin? Will not the Lord justly say to him: 'What more should I have done for you that I have not done? When you did not exist I created you, when you sinned and became the devil's slave I redeemed you, when you were going about with the wicked of this world I called you away. I let you find favor in my sight, I wanted to make my dwelling with you, and you gave me nothing but contempt. It was not my words alone that you repudiated, it was my own self, and instead you turned away in pursuit of your desires.'

But, my God, so good so tender and kind, dear friend, wise counselor, powerful support, how heartless and how rash is the man who rejects you, who casts from his heart so humble and gentle a guest! What a wretched and ruinous bargain, to accept evil and harmful thoughts in exchange for his creator, so quickly to throw open the inner chamber of the Holy Spirit, that secret place of the heart which so recently echoed with heavenly joys, to unclean thoughts, to turn it into a pig sty. Adulterous desires press in upon the heart where the footprints of the Spouse are still plain to be seen. How ill it accords, how unseemly it is, for ears which so recently listened to words which man may not utter, so quickly to attend to idle and slanderous stories, for eyes so newly purified by holy tears to turn their gaze so soon on worldly vanities, for the tongue which has scarcely ended its sweet song of welcome to the Spouse, scarcely has made peace between him and the bride with its burning and pleading eloquence, and has greeted her in the banqueting hall, to revert to foul talk, to scurrility, to lampoons and libels. Never let this happen to us, Lord, and even if we do so fall away through human frailty, never let us despair on that account, but let us hasten back to the merciful healer who lifts up the helpless ones out of the dust, and rescues the poor and wretched from the mire; for he who never desires the death of a sinner will tend us and heal us again and again.

Now it is time for us to end our letter. Let us beseech the Lord together that at this moment he will lighten the load that weighs us down so that we cannot look up to him in contemplation, and in days to come remove it altogether, leading us through these degrees from strength to strength, until we come to look upon the God of gods in Sion, where his chosen enjoy the sweetness of divine contemplation, not drop by drop, not now and then, but in an unceasing flow of delight which no one shall take away, an unchanging peace, the peace of God.

So, my brother Gervase, if it is ever granted to you from above to climb to the topmost rung of this ladder, when this happiness is yours, remember me and pray for me. So, when the veil between you and God is drawn aside, may I too see him, 'and may he who listens say to me also: Come.'

Note

Guigo II was one of the first members of the community of the Grand Chartreuse, founded in 1084 near Grenoble, France. These austere monks lived, and live, in silence, devoting themselves to meditation on the 'last things'. The Carthusians are characteristically reticent about themselves and we have few details about Guigo's life. We know only that in 1173 he was already a monk with responsibilities in the community and that in the same, or the following, year he was elected as the ninth Prior (superior) of the charterhouse. Later relieved of this responsibility, he died in 1188. We have some of his Meditations in the form of lectio divina, a Commentary on the Magnificat, and The Ladder of Monks which he wrote and dedicated to his friend Gervase, to whom he was very close for a time but apart from whom he lived. This translation of The Ladder of Monks was made by Edmond College and James Walsh and published in Guigo II: The Ladder of Monks and Twelve Meditations (Cistercian Publications 1981).

TABLE OF ABBREVIATIONS

CCSL   Corpus Christianorum, Series Latina. Turnhout: Brepols.

CF   Cistercian Fathers Series. Spencer, Massachusetts – Kalamazoo, Michigan.

CS   Cistercian Studies Series. Spencer, Massachusetts – Kalamazoo, Michigan.

PG   J.-P. Migne, Patrologia Graeca.

PL   J.-P. Migne, Patrologia Latina.

RB   The Rule of Saint Benedict.

SCh   Sources chrétiennes.

PATRISTIC AND MEDIEVAL
SOURCES IN ENGLISH

Many of the patristic and medieval works cited in the notes can be found in english translation in a number of places. Easily accessible are the series: Nicene and Ante-Nicene Fathers of the Church (NANF), Nicene and Post-Nicene Fathers of the Church (NPNF), the Fathers of the Church (FCh), Ancient Christian Writers (ACW); Cistercian Fathers (CF), Cistercian Studies (CS) Series, and the Classics of Western Spirituality (CWS). The following does not claim to be an exhaustive list.

Ambrose, *De officiis ministrorum*	*On the duties of the clergy.* The Nicene and Post-Nicene Fathers of the Church, Series II, Volume 10.
Apophthegmata patrum	*The Sayings of the Desert Fathers.* The Alphabetical Collection. Translated Benedicta Ward. CS 59.
Augustine, *Confessions*	NPNF Series 1, Volume 1; FCh, Volume 21.
Enarrationes in Psalmos	NPNF, Series 1, Volume 8.
Bernard of Clairvaux, *In Cantica Sermones*	*Sermons on the Song of Songs,* 4 volumes. CF 4, 7, 31, 40.
Gregory Nazianzen, *Oratio*	*Orations,* NPNF, Series 2, Volume 7.

Ignatius of Antioch, *Letters*	Nicene and Ante-Nicene Fathers, Volume 1.
Irenaeus of Lyons, *Adversus haereses*	NANF, Volume 1.
Jerome, *Epistolae*	*Letters*. NPNF, Series 2, Volume 6
John Chrysostom, *Sermons*	Nicene and Post-Nicene Fathers, Series I, volumes 10–14.
Origen, *In Canticum canticorum homilia*	ACW, Volume 26.

SELECTED BIBLIOGRAPHY

Since *Praying the Word* was first published in 1973, *lectio divina* as a method of prayer has been discovered by a number of Christians in various church traditions. As a result, books introducing this method of prayer have multiplied. Only works easily available in English are listed here.

Bouyer, Louis. *Introduction to Spirituality*. Translated by Mary Perkins Ryan. New York: Desclée, 1963.
———. *The Meaning of Monastic Life*. Translated by Kathleen Pond. New York: P. J. Kenedy, 1955.
Casey, Michael. *Sacred Reading: The Ancient Art of Lectio Divina*. Liguori, Missouri: Triumph Books, 1996.
Colombás, Garcia M. *Reading God*. Schuyler, Nebraska: BMH Publications, 1993.
Magrassi, Marinao. *Praying the Bible: An Introduction to Lectio Divina*. Collegeville: Liturgical Press, 1998.
De Lubac, Henri. *Medieval Exegesis: The Four Senses of Scripture*. Volume 1 [of 2]. Translated by Mark Sebanc. Grand Rapids: Eerdmans - Edinburgh: T & T Clark, 1998.
De Verteuil, Michel. *Your Word is a Light for My Steps: Lectio Divina*. Dublin: Veritas, 1996.
Havener, Ivan. *Scripture Reading of Scripture: A Guide for Beginners*. Collegeville: Liturgical Press, 1979.
Leclercq, Jean. *The Love of Learning and the Desire for God*. Translated by Catherine Misrahi. New York: Fordham University Press, 1961.
Pennington, M. Basil. *Lectio Divina: Renewing the Ancient Practice of Praying the scriptures*. New York: Crossroad, 1998.

Vest, Norvene. *Gathered in the Word.* Nashville, TN: Upper Room, 1996.

———. *Bible Reading for Spiritual Growth.* San Francisco: Harpers, 1993.

Library of Congress Cataloging-in-Publication Data

Bianchi, Enzo.
   [Pregare la Parola. English]
   Praying the Word : an introduction to Lectio divina / by Enzo
Bianchi ; translated by James W. Zona.
      p.   cm.—(Cistercian studies series ; no. 182)
   Includes bibliographical references.
   ISBN 0-87907-682-8 (pbk. : alk. paper)
   1. Bible—Devotional use.   2. Prayer—Catholic Church.
I. Series.
BS617.8.B5213   1999
248.3—dc21   98-55938
                                           CIP

CISTERCIAN TEXTS

Bernard of Clairvaux

* Apologia to Abbot William
* Five Books on Consideration: Advice to a Pope
* Homilies in Praise of the Blessed Virgin Mary
* Letters of Bernard of Clairvaux / by B.S. James
* Life and Death of Saint Malachy the Irishman
* Love without Measure: Extracts from the Writings of St Bernard / by Paul Dimier
* On Grace and Free Choice
* On Loving God / Analysis by Emero Stiegman
* Parables and Sentences
* Sermons for the Summer Season
* Sermons on Conversion
* Sermons on the Song of Songs I–IV
* The Steps of Humility and Pride

William of Saint Thierry

* The Enigma of Faith
* Exposition on the Epistle to the Romans
* Exposition on the Song of Songs
* The Golden Epistle
* The Mirror of Faith
* The Nature and Dignity of Love
* On Contemplating God: Prayer & Meditations

Aelred of Rievaulx

* Dialogue on the Soul
* Liturgical Sermons, I
* The Mirror of Charity
* Spiritual Friendship
* Treatises I: On Jesus at the Age of Twelve, Rule for a Recluse, The Pastoral Prayer
* Walter Daniel: The Life of Aelred of Rievaulx

John of Ford

* Sermons on the Final Verses of the Songs of Songs I–VII

Gilbert of Hoyland

* Sermons on the Songs of Songs I–III
* Treatises, Sermons and Epistles

Other Early Cistercian Writers

* Adam of Perseigne, Letters of
* Alan of Lille: The Art of Preaching
* Amadeus of Lausanne: Homilies in Praise of Blessed Mary
* Baldwin of Ford: Spiritual Tractates I–II
* Gertrud the Great: Spiritual Exercises
* Gertrud the Great: The Herald of God's Loving-Kindness (Books 1, 2)
* Gertrud the Great: The Herald of God's Loving-Kindness (Books 3)

* Guerric of Igny: Liturgical Sermons I
* Helinand of Froidmont: Verses on Death
* Idung of Prüfening: Cistercians and Cluniacs: The Case for Cîteaux
* Isaac of Stella: Sermons on the Christian Year, I–[II]
* The Life of Beatrice of Nazareth
* Serlo of Wilton & Serlo of Savigny: Seven Unpublished Works
* Stephen of Lexington: Letters from Ireland
* Stephen of Sawley: Treatises

MONASTIC TEXTS

Eastern Monastic Tradition

* Besa: The Life of Shenoute
* Cyril of Scythopolis: Lives of the Monks of Palestine
* Dorotheos of Gaza: Discourses and Sayings
* Evagrius Ponticus: Praktikos and Chapters on Prayer
* Handmaids of the Lord: Lives of Holy Women in Late Antiquity & the Early Middle Ages / by Joan Petersen
* Harlots of the Desert / by Benedicta Ward
* John Moschos: The Spiritual Meadow
* Lives of the Desert Fathers
* Lives of Simeon Stylites / by Robert Doran
* The Luminous Eye / by Sebastian Brock
* Mena of Nikiou: Isaac of Alexandra & St Macrobius
* Pachomian Koinonia I–III (Armand Veilleux)
* Paphnutius: Histories/Monks of Upper Egypt
* The Sayings of the Desert Fathers / by Benedicta Ward
* Spiritual Direction in the Early Christian East / by Irénée Hausherr
* The Spiritually Beneficial Tales of Paul, Bishop of Monembasia / by John Wortley
* Symeon the New Theologian: TheTheological and Practical Treatises & The Three Theological Discourses / by Paul McGuckin
* Theodoret of Cyrrhus: A History of the Monks of Syria
* The Syriac Fathers on Prayer and the Spiritual Life / by Sebastian Brock

CISTERCIAN PUBLICATIONS

TITLES LISTING

Western Monastic Tradition

- Anselm of Canterbury: Letters I–III
  / by Walter Fröhlich
- Bede: Commentary…Acts of the Apostles
- Bede: Commentary…Seven Catholic Epistles
- Bede: Homilies on the Gospels I–II
- Bede: Excerpts from the Works of St Augustine
  on the Lettrs of the Blessed Apostle Paul
- The Celtic Monk / by U. Ó Maidín
- Life of the Jura Fathers
- Maxims of Stephen of Muret
- Peter of Celle: Selected Works
- Letters of Rancé I–II
- Rule of the Master
- Rule of Saint Augustine

Christian Spirituality

- The Cloud of Witnesses: The Development
  of Christian Doctrine / by David N. Bell
- The Call of Wild Geese / by Matthew Kelty
- The Cistercian Way / by André Louf
- The Contemplative Path
- Drinking From the Hidden Fountain
  / by Thomas Špidlík
- Eros and Allegory: Medieval Exegesis of the
  Song of Songs / by Denys Turner
- Fathers Talking / by Aelred Squire
- Friendship and Community / by Brian McGuire
- Gregory the Great: Forty Gospel Homilies
- High King of Heaven / by Benedicta Word
- The Hermitage Within / by a Monk
- Life of St Mary Magdalene and of Her Sister
  St Martha / by David Mycoff
- Many Mansions / by David N. Bell
- Mercy in Weakness / by André Louf
- The Name of Jesus / by Irénée Hausherr
- No Moment Too Small / by Norvene Vest
- Penthos: The Doctrine of Compunction in the
  Christian East / by Irénée Hausherr
- Praying the Word / by Enzo Bianchi
- Rancé and the Trappist Legacy
  / by A. J. Krailsheimer
- Russian Mystics / by Sergius Bolshakoff
- Sermons in a Monastery / by Matthew Kelty
- Silent Herald of Unity: The Life of
  Maria Gabrielle Sagheddu / by Martha Driscoll
- The Spirituality of the Christian East
  / by Thomas Špidlík
- The Spirituality of the Medieval West
  / by André Vauchez
- Tuning In To Grace / by André Louf
- Wholly Animals: A Book of Beastly Tales
  / by David N. Bell

MONASTIC STUDIES

- Community and Abbot in the Rule of
  St Benedict I–II / by Adalbert de Vogüé
- The Finances of the Cistercian Order in the
  Fourteenth Century / by Peter King
- Fountains Abbey and Its Benefactors
  / by Joan Wardrop
- The Hermit Monks of Grandmont
  / by Carole A. Hutchison
- In the Unity of the Holy Spirit / by Sighard Kleiner
- The Joy of Learning & the Love of God: Essays
  in Honor of Jean Leclercq
- Monastic Odyssey / by Marie Kervingant
- Monastic Practices / by Charles Cummings
- The Occupation of Celtic Sites in Ireland
  / by Geraldine Carville
- Reading St Benedict / by Adalbert de Vogüé
- Rule of St Benedict: A Doctrinal and Spiritual
  Commentary / by Adalbert de Vogüé
- The Rule of St Benedict / by Br. Pinocchio
- St Hugh of Lincoln / by David H. Farmer
- The Venerable Bede / by Benedicta Ward
- What Nuns Read / by David N. Bell
- With Greater Liberty: A Short History of
  Christian Monasticism & Religious Orders
  / by Karl Frank

CISTERCIAN STUDIES

- Aelred of Rievaulx: A Study / by Aelred Squire
- Athirst for God: Spiritual Desire in Bernard of
  Clairvaux's Sermons on the Song of Songs
  / by Michael Casey
- Beatrice of Nazareth in Her Context
  / by Roger De Ganck
- Bernard of Clairvaux: Man, Monk, Mystic
  / by Michael Casey [tapes and readings]
- Bernardus Magister…Nonacentenary
- Catalogue of Manuscripts in the Obrecht
  Collection of the Institute of Cistercian
  Studies / by Anna Kirkwood
- Christ the Way: The Christology of Guerric of
  Igny / by John Morson
- The Cistercians in Denmark / by Brian McGuire
- The Cistercians in Scandinavia / by James France
- A Difficult Saint / by Brian McGuire
- A Gathering of Friends: Learning & Spirituality
  in John of Ford / by Costello and Holdsworth
- Image and Likeness: Augustinian Spirituality of
  William of St Thierry / by David Bell

- Index of Authors & Works in Cistercian Libraries in Great Britain I / by David Bell
- Index of Cistercian Authors and Works in Medieval Library Catalogues in Great Britian / by David Bell
- The Mystical Theology of St Bernard / by Étienne Gilson
- The New Monastery: Texts & Studies on the Earliest Cistercians
- Nicolas Cotheret's Annals of Cîteaux / by Louis J. Lekai
- Pater Bernhardus: Mentor of Martin Luther... / by Franz Posset
- A Second Look at Saint Bernard / by Jean Leclercq
- The Spiritual Teachings of St Bernard of Clairvaux / by John R. Sommerfeldt
- Studies in Medieval Cistercian History
- Studiosorum Speculum / by Louis J. Lekai
- Three Founders of Cîteaux / by Jean-Baptiste Van Damme
- Towards Unification with God (Beatrice of Nazareth in Her Context, 2)
- William, Abbot of St Thierry
- Women and St Bernard of Clairvaux / by Jean Leclercq

MEDIEVAL RELIGIOUS WOMEN

edited by Lillian Thomas Shank and John A. Nichols:
- Distant Echoes
- Hidden Springs: Cistercian Monastic Women (2 volumes)
- Peace Weavers

CARTHUSIAN TRADITION

- The Call of Silent Love / by A Carthusian
- The Freedom of Obedience / by A Carthusian
- Guigo II: The Ladder of Monks & Twelve Meditations / by Colledge & Walsh
- Halfway to Heaven / by R.B. Lockhart
- Interior Prayer / by A Carthusian
- Meditations of Guigo II / by A. Gordon Mursall
- Prayer of Love and Silence / by A Carthusian
- Poor, Therefore Rich / by A Carthusian
- They Speak by Silences / by A Carthusian
- The Way of Silent Love (A Carthusian Miscellany)
- Where Silence is Praise / by A Carthusian

- The Wound of Love (A Carthusian Miscellany)

CISTERCIAN ART, ARCHITECTURE & MUSIC

- Cistercian Abbeys of Britain
- Cistercians in Medieval Art / by James France
- Studies in Medieval Art and Architecture / edited by Meredith Parsons Lillich *(Volumes II–V are now available)*
- Stones Laid Before the Lord / by Anselme Dimier
- Treasures Old and New: Nine Centuries of Cistercian Music (compact disc)

THOMAS MERTON

- The Climate of Monastic Prayer / by T. Merton
- Legacy of Thomas Merton / by P. Hart
- Message of Thomas Merton / by P. Hart
- Monastic Journey of Thomas Merton / by P. Hart
- Thomas Merton/Monk / by P. Hart
- Thomas Merton on St Bernard
- Toward an Integrated Humanity / edited by M. Basil Pennington

CISTERCIAN LITURGICAL DOCUMENTS SERIES

- Cistercian Liturgical Documents Series / edited by Chrysogonus Waddell, ocso
- Hymn Collection of the...Paraclete
- *Institutiones nostrae:* The Paraclete Statutes
- Molesme Summer-Season Breviary (4 volumes)
- Old French Ordinary & Breviary of the Abbey of the Paraclete (2 volumes)
- Twelfth-century Cistercian Hymnal (2 volumes)
- The Twelfth-century Cistercian Psalter
- Two Early Cistercian *Libelli Missarum*

STUDIA PATRISTICA

- Studia Patristica XVIII, Volumes I, 2 and 3

CISTERCIAN PUBLICATIONS

HOW TO CONTACT US

Editorial Queries

Editorial queries & advance book information
should be directed to the Editorial Offices:

• Cistercian Publications
  WMU Station
  1201 Oliver Street
  Kalamazoo, Michigan 49008

• Telephone   616 387 8920
• Fax   616 387 8921

How to Order in the United States

Customers may order these books through
booksellers or directly by contacting the
warehouse at the address below:

• Cistercian Publications
  Saint Joseph's Abbey
  167 North Spencer Road
  Spencer, Massachusetts 01562-1233

• Telephone   508 885 8730
• Fax   508 885 4687
• e-mail   cistpub@spencerabbey.org
• Web Site   www.spencerabbey.org/cistpub

How to Order from Canada

• Novalis
  49 Front Street East, Second Floor
  Toronto, Ontario M5E 1B3

• Telephone   416 363 3303
              1 800 387 7164
• Fax   416 363 9409

How to Order from Europe

• Cistercian Publications
  Mount Saint Bernard Abbey
  Coalville, Leicester LE67 5UL

• Fax   44 1530 81 46 08

Cistercian Publications is a non-profit corporation. Its publishing program is restricted to monastic texts in translation and books on the monastic tradition.

A complete catalogue of texts in translation and studies on early, medieval, and modern monasticism is available, free of charge, from any of the addresses above.